Peer-Mediated Instruction

Peer-Mediated Instruction

PETER S. ROSENBAUM

Teachers College, Columbia University

Teachers College Press
Teachers College, Columbia University
New York and London

To Irma V. Thurman

Contents

Introduction   1

Chapter 1
CAI Origins   17

Chapter 2
The First PMI System   39

Chapter 3
From Special to General Purpose   66

Chapter 4
The Experiment   83

Chapter 5
An In-Service Application: The Jackson PMI Project   105

Chapter 6
Observations and Reflections   149

PMI/MS Manual   165

Acknowledgments   276

About the Author   278

Two are better than one. . . . For
if they fall, the one will lift up his
fellow; but woe to him that is alone
when he falleth; for he hath not
another to help him up.

ECCLESIASTES

Introduction

The Issue

Teaching is ultimately the act of guiding someone through a network of planned experiences with the hope that in the process the learner will somehow develop means for coping with novel experiences. Ideal guidance is guidance that does not permit the learner to stray from the paths of relevant experience. Guidance thus implies sensitivity to the circumstances of the learner and the power to alter these circumstances; in short, guidance means *control*.

"Control" is a hard word; it conjures notions of mind control, the total control of the Skinner Box, political control, media control, force. But the term also implies deliberation, consideration, judgment, power, foresight, efficiency, support; in short, the combination of traits that human civilization depends upon. It is the sense of control embodied by these latter concepts that underpins this discussion. It is the control of man the tool maker, who uses his intelligence to apply his understanding of how nature works to the solution of problems that he or his social group is experiencing. It is also the control of man the ship's captain, who orchestrates the use of his tools and resources with maximal effect in the face of adverse circumstances. Finally, it is the control of man the teacher, who acts upon the environment of the

1

learner in such a manner as to maximize for the learner the appropriateness, timeliness, and potency of environmental stimulation.

In any particular instructional setting, ideal control is never achieved—that is, the controller always lacks to some extent in the ability either to sense the circumstances of the learner or to intervene with maximum **Ideal** appropriateness. For example, in a system of instruction **instructional** employing printed books, the decentralized manner of **control is** the book's use sets much of the learner's experience **never** beyond the direct control of the teacher, with a con- **achieved.** sequent reduction in the potency of instructional control, as noted by Edward L. Thorndike in his analysis of print technology.*

> If, by a miracle of mechanical ingenuity, a book could be so arranged that only to him who had done what was directed on page one would page two become visible, and so on, much that now requires personal instruction could be managed by print.

Since instructional control costs money, however, the critical measure of the instructional control function is not the extent of the discrepancy between actual performance and ideal performance, but the efficiency of the performance relative to desired instructional ends. Thus, when an instructional control scheme is invented whereby decentralized (i.e., individualized) learning is centrally verified through public examination, there comes into existence an instructional control function that is far from ideal but that may in operation prove to be enormously productive. Indeed, this is the essence of the mechanism of instructional control that has served throughout Western culture for the past three hundred years or so wherever the purchase of books for individual use in instruction has been economically possible.

Until recently the public schools of the United States have been able to conduct their affairs and carry out their various functions in a manner that has not occasioned any special concern for the current viability of the now

---

* Edward L. Thorndike, *Education: A First Book* (New York: Macmillan, 1912), p. 165.

traditional method of instructional control. Within the
past ten years, however, two circumstances have come
into view that converge on this issue and apparently
are beginning to generate pressures likely to bring instructional control into focus as a high priority candi-
date for technological development. The first circumstance is simply that the costs of traditional instruction
are apparently reaching the limit of what the financial
supporters of the schools are predisposed to pay. The
currency of such terms as "behavioral objectives," "accountability," "performance contracting," "continuous
progress instruction," all terms of recent vintage, some
already jaded, is not coincidental, for they all reflect
the current urgent interest in the technologizing of instructional control for the express purpose of minimizing
the costs of instruction with respect to desired educational ends. The second circumstance is the growing
realization that conventional instructional methodology
simply fails to be effective for large segments of the
school population. No clearer example can be cited than
the Federal Right to Read program, which officially
recognizes that conventional schooling techniques have
not worked well in the skills of reading and explicitly
accepts the necessity of inventing and implementing new
approaches to instruction in this area. In short, conventional methods of instructional control are, in critical instances of great social importance, failing to achieve
desired results. In all instances, these methods are already
costing too much. Both factors are likely to prove of
sufficient import to justify the development of an improved technology of instructional control.

Conventional pedagogy costs too much.

Conventional pedagogy doesn't work very well.

It may seem from these considerations that the problem could be viewed as an economic one, one of getting
enough teachers to achieve the necessary closeness of
observation and interaction with the student. However,
the economics of lessening the student-teacher ratio
obviously precludes this as a promising approach to the
improvement of instructional control on any large scale.
Rather, a less recalcitrant problem is to reach a key technical goal in the matter of instructional design, to find

The heart of the design problem. cost efficient means of collecting and processing behavioral data and using them to achieve effective direction of student activity with an absolute minimum of teacher time. The purpose of this book is to present and explain one approach to the solution of this problem.

The Design Problem

First, it is important to recognize that instructional control is implemented not as a thing, a monolithic entity, but as a *system,* that is, a set whose elements belong together because they function interdependently; **The necessity of a system concept.** they cooperate. Thorndike's "miracle of mechanical ingenuity," a book so arranged that "only to him who had done what was directed on page one would page two become visible," would demand a system design capable of executing two interdependent functions. First, the system would have to be capable of regulating the display (i.e., flow) of textual material to the student. Second, the system would somehow have to engage the student behaviorally in such a manner as to determine the point at which the student had achieved mastery of a particular quantum of material. The effect should be that when the student is performing at a level below the criterion level, his activities would be directed toward achievement of criterion level performance; when this level of performance is reached (either because of true improvement in performance or because a higher level control decision has been made to lower the criterion threshold), the student would be given access to new material. In this manner, exposure to new material, "the next page" in Thorndike's sense, is made absolutely contingent upon how well the student is doing with the material he is currently working on. To achieve such an effect, the student, the materials, the monitoring apparatus, the display apparatus for a system, all would have to work together as a system.

Assuming for the moment that a structure for such an instructional control system can be conceived and given form, a second equally crucial aspect of the design problem emerges—the question of whether the hardware and software components as conceived during the design process can be reconciled with the merciless demands of the marketplace. Of these, economic viability is the most obvious. Two such measures of viability are pertinent. The first is the *absolute cost* of the system, which includes the cost of the *fixed* components of the system, e.g., hardware and non-consumable software, and of the *changing* components, most notably instructional staff and consumable items. The second measure of economic viability is cost relative to benefits derived, e.g., *efficiency*. Whereas absolute cost pertains to establishing alternatives, cost relative to benefits pertains to making selections among otherwise acceptable alternatives.

The demands of the marketplace.

Both measures relate closely to the design process itself, but the latter more essentially than the former, for the concept of efficiency creates a criterion of adequacy with which to decide on competing alternative solutions to the same problem. For example, in Thorndike's scheme the goal is to ensure total subject matter mastery for all students, limited presumably by variability in I.Q. and motivation. Thus, the concept of efficiency will deal with the utilization of the cost-bearing components of the system in the process of achieving specific learning goals. An instructional control system approaches the ideal as it maximizes the productivity of its cost-bearing components. A good system strives to ensure that the activities in which students participate are maximally appropriate to the attainment of whatever the instructional objectives may be. It economizes in the use of staff time. It maximizes the "thru-put" of fixed components, and so forth.

Efficiency as a measure of viability.

Another equally critical demand of the marketplace has to do with *acceptance* of the system as a whole by those in the school who are being asked to be part of the system and to cooperate in making it work. Most commonly, this means students, teachers, and supervisory personnel. In every sense, an instructional control system is a *product*, and is subject, as such, to the same vagaries. The manufacturer of home appliances develops his product conceptions within a detailed understanding of what goes on in the home. His products are intended

Product acceptance as a measure of viability.

to facilitate certain well-defined, carefully delineated tasks. The same observation could be made about the manufacturer of office products. In both instances, the products are conceived with the hope that they will be clearly recognized by the consumer as *system facilitators* and, as such, will be valued highly enough to be purchased at the price offered. Examples of system facilitators are numerous and obvious—copying machines, adding machines, sewing machines, etc.

A product that is intended by its manufacturer to be functional, but which is not seen by its prospective buyer as facilitating some process in which he is in some way engaged, is a product that will not be purchased. If a product is purchased, but when put into use neither makes life easier nor provides compensatory rewards, the use of the product will be discontinued. Or perhaps, the product will be "misused," that is, used in some improvised manner especially conceived by the user. There has been a great deal of product development in education that has ended in failure, even though the specific products have often shown a certain flair for inventiveness. These failures have often been held by manufacturers as testimony to the technical and even emotional incompetence of school personnel. But this point of view is no more productive than attributing the sales failure of a new dishwasher to incompetence in housewifery, for it misses the fundamental point of systems design: the adequacy of any subsystem is dependent upon its compatibility with the global system in which it is to be integrated. The ultimate test of any scheme for implementing an instructional control system is whether it can successfully be integrated within the existing patterns of life in the schools.

The Approach

There exist several general conceptions of instructional control, each possessing varying degrees of associated immediate practical utility. The most ambitious conception might be called the *complete customization conception,* in which it is taken as desirable to be able to as-

Complete customization.

certain in comprehensive detail the cognitive make-up of a learner and, armed with such information, to be able to tailor a total, ordered inventory of learning experiences leading to specific objectives. At the present time, the scientific understanding and technical skill that would be required to achieve this goal, even were there to be agreement on its desirability, neither exist nor are being rapidly approached.

A less ambitious conception, in fact a component of the complete customization conception, is the *proficiency profiling conception*, which assumes that the learning program for any one student should be tailored to his current state of understanding and proficiency. Proficiency profiling is implicit in the concept of diagnostic teaching, in the placement of students on the basis of pretesting, hopefully with the result that students will come into contact exclusively with relevant instructional material at the correct level of difficulty. This concept is more feasible than the previous one in that it can be carried out in at least a primitive fashion. The full promise of proficiency profiling as an instructional control technique, however, will involve developing powerful means to measure the current state of knowledge of a learner and implies a program with massive and complex instructional resources.

Proficiency profiling.

A considerably less formidable concept to realize is the *Thorndike conception* implicit in his "miracle of mechanical ingenuity." In this conception the nature and content of the learning tasks may be essentially the same, or in any event finite, for all learners. Instructional control is achieved by allowing the learner to proceed at his own pace; by highlighting for him the discrepancies between his own performance and the ideal performance; by regulating the quantity of work he will be required to do in each subject matter area on the basis of a quantitative estimate of his proficiency with respect to the instructional goals of the program; and perhaps by supplementing the main line of learning activities with remedial or motivational material. Notwithstanding the long-term promise of the complete customization and proficiency profiling conceptions of instructional control,

Thorndike's conception.

the Thorndike conception is not only a demonstrably powerful one, but one that is feasible both technically and economically right now, and for this reason has been the focus of the work to be reported on herein.

The aforementioned conceptions might be thought of as leading to only one of the possible goals of instruction, namely, that for a given time and effort the student should learn as much as possible as judged by customary measures of achievement. There exists a contrasting view of learning outcomes, one that seeks to achieve more qualitative and less tangible goals. This is the *learner-directed approach* to instruction, in which the learner is given a significant degree of control over the order, content, and even purposes of his learning program. As a possible outcome, it is hoped that the student will have a better understanding and retention of those things he has learned through his work, that emphasis on meaning and purposes in the learning activity and on formulation and achievement of goals may give the student a broad perspective of the interrelationships of the things he knows, and insight into how he develops mastery of a new area so that he will develop a general ability to learn, a problem solving set toward his work, and habituation to self-direction and initiative.

Learner-directed instruction.

The learner-directed approach should not be taken to imply the blatant inefficiency of putting the student entirely on his own either in designing or in carrying out his learning program; as one of my teachers used to say, "it is a great deficiency of the school of hard knocks that the graduates are too old to work." From the standpoint of instructional systems design, ordinary group instruction differs from learner-directed instruction in the degree to which attention must be devoted to the supervision of student learning activity. Whatever the potential of the learner-directed approach may be, its success will depend upon achieving a quality of instructional control superior to what is currently realized in group instruction. Thus, for a fixed student-teacher ratio, the teacher will find that, in the case of learner-directed activity, it is more demanding, indeed often impossible, to follow what is happening and to recognize the need for teacher intervention in such activity than in the case of teacher-directed activity. This consideration signals all the more the potential value of pursuing the development of the Thorndike conception of instructional control.

The Background

It is no longer visionary to contemplate an implementation of the kind of instructional control system that Thorndike seemed to be hinting at. One such is the IPI (Individually Prescribed Instruction) system generally associated with Robert Glaser and his associates at the University of Pittsburgh. Another is Project PLAN, developed collaboratively by Westinghouse Learning Corporation and American Institutes for Research under the guidance of John Flanagan. In both schemes, there is a task emphasis in learning; children go through the school by carrying out complete assignments, a single one of which may take the student an hour or so. The student normally carries each task through to completion. At the conclusion of a task the student shows that he has finished the job successfully by passing some simple test. When a student does badly on a test, he is given more learning exercises from the same unit until he can master it successfully. The essential point in both systems pertains to how the student's behavior is evaluated and how evaluation is used to control the running of the system. Evaluation is oriented toward prescription; the purpose of taking a test is to determine what a student will do next, not whether he has passed or failed. Thus, the contingencies in the system, that is, the outcomes that depend upon what a student does, are related to the student's achievements; and the consequences are the student's next task assignments. When evaluation is used for the purpose of making instructional prescriptions for students, it may be regarded as adhering to a philosophy of proficiency-oriented instruction, or, as it is occasionally put, mastery instruction.

Various schemes currently do exist.

IPI and PLAN schoolrooms are somewhat chaotic in appearance, with individuals moving hither and thither,

going about their own business as the system may prescribe. Students have to be able to accept and exercise considerable responsibility for supervising themselves.
They therefore have to be aware of where they are, what
they are doing, and when they are going to do it. For that
reason, IPI and PLAN should represent a very good
way to train students in responsibility for their own
behavior. Such schools should exert a strong force on
students to develop good work patterns, good character
traits, good self-confidence based upon successful experiences with coping. Such instructional systems might
well provide superior preparation for effectiveness in
adult life.

On the negative side, both IPI and PLAN are *special-
purpose* systems; they have an extremely limited range
of applicability. That is, quite aside from questions of
cost (and PLAN has had a considerable per pupil cost
associated with its use), these systems demand major
pedagogical concessions from the school. In both instances, a fixed immutable set of behavioral objectives
is built into the system. Further, in the case of IPI, e.g.,
IPI-Math, the content of instruction is fixed as well.

Limitations of PLAN and IPI. Thus, a school that wishes to use IPI-Math must not only
accept a specific set of behavioral objectives, but also a
specific set of materials as well. It is like buying a television set that is pre-wired to accept one, and only one,
channel. PLAN is one step more general than IPI in that,
although it is based upon a fixed set of behavioral objectives, it specifically permits the instructional materials
Both are special-purpose systems. to vary. The PLAN system has the capability of refer-
encing existing materials of instruction. Neither system,
however, is general purpose in the sense of allowing
variable behavioral objectives.

But why is it desirable that an instructional control
system accommodate alternate and even incompatible
behavioral objectives? For one thing, it is no simple job
to define behavioral objectives that are generally acceptable. Not only do regional differences exist in the
goals of instruction; even regarding the basics, there
exists great disagreement regarding definitions, sequences, and priorities. But even were we assured that

in some number of years hence there would exist a uniform set of objectives, this would in no way advance the cause of improved instructional control today. Today, there exist in the schools at least as many different (although partially overlapping) sets of behavioral objectives as there are different textbooks with different tables of contents. Therefore, if improved instructional control is desirable at all, what is most urgently needed is a general technique of instructional control that can apply directly and without delay to variable sets of behavioral objectives as they *currently exist* in the schools.

An ideal system accommodates variable instructional objectives.

In this connection, the most intriguing technical development is the *flexible programing* approach to computer-assisted instruction (CAI).

In the sense that is most relevant to the present discussion, CAI is a term referring to a two-way communications system between a learner and a computer in which the computer can, in principle, *attend* to messages from the learner (generally typed by the learner on a typewriter-like console) and can, on the basis of that input, *decide* on an appropriate response to the learner. Under the flexible programing approach to CAI, the vendor provides the user with CAI hardware *and* a CAI operating system. The latter makes it possible for the user to write computer programs (as in IBM's Coursewriter series) that will cause specific interactions to occur between the student and the computer when the student sits down at the instructional console. For example, it would be well within the state of the art to write a CAI computer program that Thorndike would have accepted as his "miracle of mechanical ingenuity." To wit, in a conventional classroom, operating under a conventional set of mechanics, a student writes out his exercises in a workbook, or some facsimile thereof. All too frequently, the student will receive only minimal feedback on his efforts. If corrected at all, the student's work will as likely as not only be marked "right" or "wrong," and even then will be returned long after the student's paper has ceased to be of any interest to him. With computer-assisted instruction conceived as a responsive workbook system, however, the student would key in his responses

The implementation of Thorndike.

on a typewriter-like console, which would respond *immediately* with a corrective or advisory message tailored (how closely depending upon the sophistication of the computer program) to the characteristics of the student's performance. Specifically, the responsive workbook would watch for performance errors in real-time, would signal to the student when an error has been detected, would show him where the error occurred, and would give him the opportunity to improve his performance, right then and there. Under a conventional methodology, some students never get enough practice to allow them to achieve minimum desirable performance levels, because, quite simply, the texts contain insufficient amounts of material. Other students are required to cover more material than is actually necessary, for no convenient mechanism exists to establish when the student has mastered the topic. A responsive workbook system, however, would, on the basis of a continuously updated assessment of a student's performance, adjust the amount of work required of that student according to individual need. Thus, the student's advancement through the course of study would become directly related to his performance.

CAI as a "responsive workbook."

The essence of the flexible programing approach to CAI lies in the fact that the user, i.e., the school, is provided not with pre-written completed courses of instruction, ready to run on his machine, but with a programing language for creating his own courses. IBM's Coursewriter programing language makes possible the use of a small universe of options to conceive and implement CAI instructional programs in all subject matters and at all grade levels. Thus, this particular conception of CAI holds out the prospect of effective *general purpose* instructional control.

Computer-assisted instruction can provide the desired flexibility.

In the most immediately relevant sense, it is academic to project that CAI of any kind offers a generally applicable short-term answer to the instructional control problem, because of the current excessive cost of computer systems. Even were cost not a factor, however, the probability of success for the flexible programing concept of CAI would have to be questioned. The intellectual, technical, and emotional demands of Coursewriter "authoring" are almost without parallel in contemporary American teaching procedures and practices, with the only exception being textbook authoring, a design activity that falls outside the domain of interest for all but a few teachers. Between Coursewriter and the school practitioner, there exists a culture gap. It is to be hoped that school personnel will respond favorably to a well-designed and fully-formed instructional control system accommodating variable instructional objectives, but *merely the tools* to invent such a system, which is what flexible programing CAI offers, is something the school practitioner neither needs, nor wants, nor is able to use at the present time.

CAI is not a promising short-term prospect.

The Purpose of This Book

All of which brings me to the purpose of this book, which is to illuminate a rather different kind of attempt to find a design solution to Thorndike's problem, but one that has led to a conception and implementation of one class of instructional control systems about which a number of interesting things can be said. Four of these are very important.

1. The system was specifically conceived to provide for variability in behavioral objectives and instructional content.
2. It can be implemented with relative ease by school personnel.
3. It is highly effective.
4. It can be implemented at virtually zero incremental cost.

It may be interesting that this system had its origin as an unusual type of computer simulation, not, as in the more common case, a simulation of some real-world system by a computer, but a simulation of a computerized instructional control system by the teachers and students in a school. This system was an outgrowth of my participation in the CAI work of Edward N. Adams and his associates at IBM Research; it was initially conceived as a way to achieve zero-cost CAI.

The system is called Peer-Mediated Instruction.

The Story Line

Part One

The story begins in the IBM Research Division at Yorktown Heights, New York, where, as Manager of the Language Learning Group in the Computers in Education Department, I received my first exposure to computer-assisted instruction. At the time of my entry into the Department, the Research Group was engaged in the second year of a large-scale study of CAI's effectiveness in the first-year German course at the State University of New York, Stony Brook. The experimental results that had been achieved during the first year of the study were seen to strongly favor the CAI treatment. Since it was nominally a primary responsibility of my job to conceive, develop, and assess CAI applications in the language instruction area, I found myself meditating a great deal about why the Stony Brook CAI should have worked as well as it did. After all, a cursory examination of the CAI literature and the field in general could only lead one to the conclusion that CAI is not magic. It is just as easy to have a CAI failure as a CAI success, perhaps easier. By a process of elimination, I gradually convinced myself that a number of possible causes were most unlikely: the literal course content as it was manifest in the textbooks upon which the CAI course was based; the sequencing of the content; the pedagogical plan of the textbooks that were used in the course; the pedagogical qualifications of the instructors with whom students had contact; fascination on the part of students with the CAI hardware proper; special student aptitude; extraordinary motivational factors. Increasingly, I came to suspect that the success of the CAI application had very little to do with the CAI hardware *per se,* but a very great deal to do with the method of interaction between student and computer that the computer program had caused to exist. It gradually became clear that, in certain apparently crucial respects, this CAI interaction was simulating the kind of instructional transaction that would take place between a student and a good teacher. In other words, the CAI program had in effect isolated certain key features of successful language instruction, indeed skills instruction in general, and had, by virtue of the intensification of instructional experience that CAI in general makes possible, greatly augmented the student's exposure to these features; hence the impressive, but now not so surprising, instructional gains.

During the course of these speculations, an idea occurred to me, of which the work reported in this book is the fruit: Assuming that my analysis of the causes of CAI's efficacy in the Stony Brook study was essentially correct, might it not be possible to devise a special *buddy system* interaction that would simulate these causes, thereby achieving similar, conceivably even greater, instructional gains at low cost? In other words, might it not be possible for one student to simulate the computer for his peer?

Part Two

The first attempts to create a system of peer-mediated instruction were carried forth at Teachers College, Columbia University, where I joined the faculty with the specific intention of pursuing the line of research that had begun at IBM. I chose to work with the subject matter of spelling for a number of reasons. In the first place, spelling is a fairly well defined and contained subject matter. It would thus be a simple matter to piece together an experimental application with a specific objective, namely to teach the correct spelling of a certain number of words. Second, it seemed to me that spelling skill is one that benefits from the kind of intensive practice the IBM version of CAI had to offer; thus, there was good reason to believe that if a system of CAI simulation via peer mediation could work at all, it would work for spelling. Third, there existed an apparent need for viable methods that could improve the quality of spelling instruction.

Over a period of several months, I, along with a number of students, devised prototype materials, working frequently with elementary school students who had been "borrowed" from their regular classes in pairs. Ultimately, when it began to become clear that peer mediation could, given appropriate constraints on design, work smoothly, the entire system was given a test at P.S. 129 in Manhattan. The results were sufficiently impressive to convince all of those who worked on the project that we could, with strong justification, proceed to the design, development, and performance testing of a large-scale general purpose system of instructional control based upon peer mediation.

Part Three

The opportunity to create a general purpose peer-mediated instructional control system arose in connection with a query from American Telephone and Telegraph Company about the possibility of devising an instructional control system to use in its operating divisions for instruction in remedial reading. This query led to a period of intensive collaboration in which a group at Teachers College designed such a system and tested its effectiveness and efficiency in the context of a basic skills training environment of the New York Telephone Company. The reader is left to assess the results of the New York Telephone study himself. May I simply preview these results by saying that the differential effects observed were not merely of statistical significance; they were large, by any standards of evaluating instructional methods with which I am familiar, and hence of potentially great practical significance; in other words, the proper use of Peer-Mediated Instruction can lead to the quantitative and qualitative benefits that are to be hoped for from improving the quality of control in instruction.

Part Four

Do-It-Yourself! (An account of a remedial reading project conducted by the Jackson Public Schools, Jackson, Mississippi.)

CHAPTER 1

CAI Origins

The IBM CAI Research Group

Over a period of years in the mid-1960's, the IBM Corporation invested several million dollars in developmental research on the educational technology that has come to be known as computer-assisted instruction (CAI). To my way of thinking, the most creative mind in this research enterprise was Edward N. Adams, a theoretical physicist by training, a manager of engineering activities by vocation, and a man with a penchant for education as clear and as strong and as honest as Edward L. Thorndike's, to whose philosophical views Adams' bear a great likeness.

Edward N. Adams of IBM.

Nominally, it was the mission of Adams' CAI Group to conceive, develop, and test CAI applications, and in so doing to discover the particular values that might inhere in a merger between time-shared computing and the instructional process. Characteristically, Adams' investigations were carried out within the framework of large-scale cooperative ventures linking the IBM CAI Group, of which I was a member during certain critical phases, with the instructional and curricular staffs of educational institutions. The academic people would supply curricular expertise; the IBM Group would supply the CAI hardware and software and, via the latter, the pedagogical design as it was implicit in the form of the dialogue by which student and computer would communicate

17

during the CAI learning process. Adams approached the creation of CAI computer programs as an analytic engineer, each new program intending to confirm design hypotheses and striving to attain ideal goals.

Adams' Group carried out CAI research in a number of subject matter areas at various grade levels, including elementary school arithmetic, college statistics, college physics, and college foreign language instruction. Of these, foreign language instruction was accorded the greatest attention over the longest period of time, for it was felt that, given the state of CAI hardware and system technology, this subject matter offered an especially favorable instructional situation for exploiting and validating CAI instructional control technology.

An excursion into foreign language instruction.

CAI Language Instruction

In what ways was foreign language instruction of special interest and promise? To begin with, certain features of successful foreign language instruction impose heavy burdens upon language teaching programs and upon language teachers. In particular, a great investment of classroom time must be made in the supervision of interactive practice. Estimates of the amount of classroom time actually devoted to this activity can run as high as 60% for basic courses, and rarely less than 40%. So much interactive work is used because it is thought, correctly, that the student cannot supervise his own foreign language practice effectively; it has to be supervised by a teacher who is a competent speaker of the language being learned. It is thought that the foreign language student left to his own devices may not be aware that he has made an error, or he may not know where his error occurred, or what it was. Consequently, for whatever reason, the student will not successfully correct or improve his performance.

Even when a teacher gives careful personal supervision to classroom activity, it is generally understood that time spent in group practice is not maximally efficient for language learning. The problem is simply one of conserving real time. In a basic language course of fifteen students, the typical number of linguistic interactions (a back-and-forth pair of utterances between two people) between a teacher and a particular student—in a fifty-minute class—will not exceed four or five. In an entire two-semester first-year course, therefore, a student in this class will participate in no more than four or five hundred foreign language interchanges, a figure that compares very unfavorably with the frequency with which we interchange sentences in our native language. So, even though a great deal of classroom time may be devoted to individualized practice, the individual student typically doesn't get much. *Not much time for practice.*

A study conducted by the East Slavic Division of the Defense Language Institute–West Coast and summarized in Figure 1 illustrates this point well. In a typical DLI class of nine students, each student will actively participate in the foreign language for only 3.6 minutes out of a fifty-minute class. In a more typical college class of fifteen students, active participation time would diminish to something like 1.7 minutes.

In a CAI setting, a student interacts with the subject matter via a special computer controlled student station, called a *terminal,* which responds to what the student types on a keyboard. Since each student has his own terminal, the student may readily experience forty or fifty interactions in a fifty-minute session, about ten times as many as he would normally engage in during a typical classroom hour. This observation gave us reason to hope that the effectiveness of foreign language practice could be improved through the use of CAI as an adjunct to a foreign language class. *The CAI solution.*

Intensification.

Pedagogical Decisions

The effectiveness of foreign language CAI would depend not only on the quantity of interactions, but also on the appropriateness of these interactions to the subject matter being learned. Language instruction experts have devised numerous language learning tasks for use in face-to-face exercises. Some of these were potentially suitable for the CAI laboratory. We felt that, to be

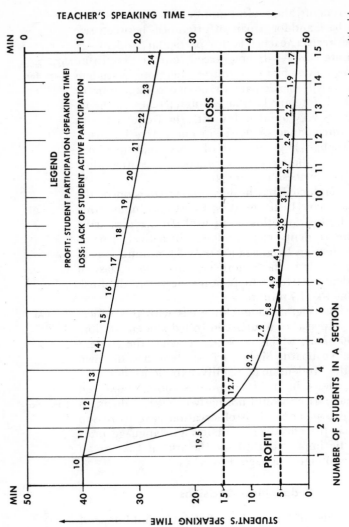

Figure 1. The amount of time available for an individual student to interact in class with his instructor (at DLI–West Coast) as a function of the number of students in the class. (This chart was given to me through the kindness of Mr. Alex Albov, Chairman of the East Slavic Division, Defense Language Institute–West Coast, Monterey, California.)

Think of the public school class with twenty to thirty students.

promising for CAI use, an exercise should satisfy two essential criteria. First, we believed that a language learning task should require the student to take a creative action in the target language, i.e., either to *generate* (rather than *select from a known set*) an utterance or to produce a response based on comprehension of an utterance. Generative tasks are important because they are closely related to the desired objectives of foreign language instruction. A person who knows a foreign language is one who can comprehend and produce the utterances of that language.

A second criterion for a potentially valuable exercise type was that it call forth behaviors that employ the critical components of the subject matter. One component of linguistic knowledge consists of knowing how the sentences of the language are constructed, what the words mean, and how the meaning of sentences is extracted from sentence structures. The now common term for this kind of knowledge is *linguistic competence.* The second aspect of linguistic knowledge involves the ability actually to construct and comprehend the sentences of the language in speaking, listening, reading, and writing. These are *performance skills.* In our research, we sought generative exercise types that would address both linguistic competence and performance.

Here is a partial inventory of some of the exercises the CAI Group implemented for experimental use:

1. *Substitution-Transformation.* The student is presented (via typewriter or TV screen) with a base sentence. Appearing below this sentence are either single words or constituents. The student's task is to generate (type in) the sentence that would result from the substitution of these words or constituents into the base sentence. In a variant of this exercise, the student receives the material to be substituted aurally via a computer-controlled tape recorder.

2. *Cue Transformation.* The student is presented with a base sentence. A cue appears below this sentence; for example, the word *interrogative.* The task is to transform the base sentence according to the cue.

3. *Analogical Transformation.* The student is pre-

sented with a pair of sentences, the second a transform of the first. He is then presented with a third sentence, which has the same pattern as the first. His task is to generate the transform of the third sentence analogically to the first pair of sentences.

4. *Translation.* The student is presented with an utterance in his own language, perhaps also with some constraining instructions; he must render the meaning of the utterance into the target language subject to the constraint. Translation is a non-paradigmatic exercise, unlike the exercise types mentioned previously. That is, if a particular lesson were to contain a number of small isolated grammatical points that could not be practiced economically in a paradigmatic fashion, then a translation sentence or two could be employed to address the topic. Also, translation permits vocabulary practice.

These four types of exercises address the domain of linguistic competence efficiently and comprehensively; they also influence the performance skills of reading, writing, and listening, since these are the media in which the student practices. The IBM Group expected that in doing these exercises students would acquire performance abilities as well as linguistic competence.

Among the exercises appropriate primarily for performance skills are dictation and aural comprehension.

5. *Dictation.* Here, the student is given an aural stimulus, which may be a sentence, a group of numbers, a group of names, or a group of vocabulary items. The student's task is to write what he hears. Dictation, especially sentence dictation, provides good practice in aural discrimination, including stress and intonation; it exercises and tests orthography; and it strengthens the student's understanding of the relationship between spoken and written form.

6. *Aural Comprehension.* In a typical aural comprehension exercise, the student will listen to a brief dialogue; he will then be asked questions about it. This exercise is a good one for training a student in the ability not only to perceive but to understand, since in order to perform the task required, he *must* understand and must listen more and more intently until he does so.

These, then, are a few exercise types that are creative and that address aspects of linguistic competence and performance. In its first large-scale experiment with CAI in foreign language instruction, the CAI Group implemented exercises drawn from this set.

The Stony Brook Study

In 1966, the CAI Research Group entered an intensive period of collaboration with the language instruction staff at the State University of New York at Stony Brook.* In its second year, this collaboration centered on a large-scale control study involving Stony Brook's first year German course and its roughly 250 students over two academic semesters, and intended to provide a quantitative comparison between IBM's CAI methodology and the more-or-less conventional audio-lingual methodology at that time in use at Stony Brook. Quoting Adams' write-up in his "Field Evaluation . . .":

An experiment is established.

The operational evaluation of the lab was a comparison of the performances of 109 CAI subjects and 141 audio-lingual subjects, all of the first year German students at the Stony Brook campus in the 1967-1968 year. The students for the experimental group were chosen by chance through the normal routine of registration. There was no special training for the staff, nor special efforts to influence the teachers' instructional styles for teaching the experimental course except that the teachers were instructed to use audio-lingual methods in class and to teach no reading and writing in class.

All groups were compared on the basis of initial aptitude, final proficiencies on each of four skills, attrition rate during

* The Stony Brook project is documented in the following articles: E. N. Adams, H. W. Morrison, and J. M. Reddy, "Conversation With a Computer as a Technique of Language Instruction," *The Modern Language Journal*, Vol. VII, No. 1 (January 1968), pp. 3-16; F. A. Ruplin and J. R. Russell, "A Type of Computer Assisted Instruction," *The German Quarterly*, Vol. XVI, No. 1 (January 1968), pp. 84-88; H. W. Morrison and E. N. Adams, "Pilot Study of a CAI Laboratory in German," *Computer-Assisted Instruction*, Richard Atkinson and H. W. Wilson, eds. (New York: Academic Press, 1969), pp. 199-204; E. N. Adams, "Field Evaluation of the German CAI Lab," *ibid.*, pp. 205-208.

the year, attitudes toward instructional method, and ability at year-end to gain advanced placement. The Modern Language Association Aptitude Test was used to compare the initial aptitude distributions of the students in the two groups; the distributions were closely similar, as is shown in Figure 2. Attrition during the year was about the same percent in both groups, a bit over 30%, which is typical of first year German at Stony Brook. The attitudes of both teachers and students toward the CAI laboratory were quite positive.

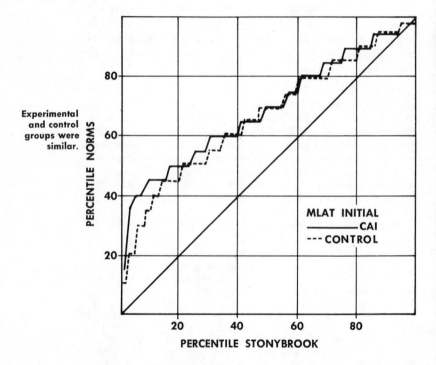

Figure 2. Initial distribution of scores on the Modern Language Aptitude Test.

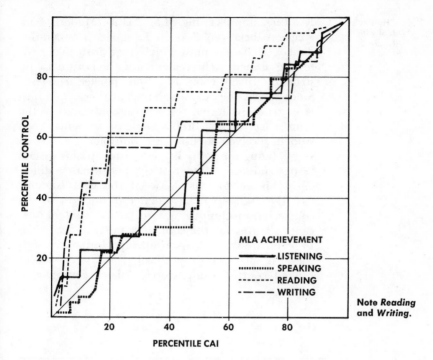

Figure 3. Distribution of proficiencies on the four components of the MLA Foreign Language Cooperative Test. The percentile rank of a CAI Group raw score is plotted as the percentile rank in the Control (Audio-Lingual) Group that the same score would have achieved.

Adams presented the performance outcomes of this experiment in a single chart, which is replicated as Figure 3 above. To fully appreciate this chart, there are a few things one must know about how foreign language achievement is tested and about how this graph was constructed.

1. In its elementary phases of accomplishment, foreign language learning is pictured as consisting of four component sub-skills: Listening, Speaking,

**How to
deal with
Figure 3.**
Reading, and Writing. The MLA (Modern Language Association) Foreign Language Cooperative Test, perhaps the most widely used instrument for testing student achievement after exposure to instruction, itself comprises four labeled sub-tests. Since it was this set of sub-tests that was administered as the criterion test at year end to all of the "surviving" Stony Brook German students, each student received not one score, but four.

2. In analyzing the Stony Brook results, Adams wished to determine the extent of the performance differences known to exist between the CAI students and the audio-lingual students at the end of the course. His technique was to create a set of percentile norms for the control population and then to compare the CAI group's performance with these norms. More specifically, for each set of ranked control group scores, Adams computed a

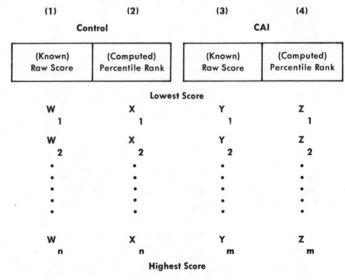

(1)	(2)	(3)	(4)
Control		**CAI**	
(Known) Raw Score	(Computed) Percentile Rank	(Known) Raw Score	(Computed) Percentile Rank
		Lowest Score	
W_1	X_1	Y_1	Z_1
W_2	X_2	Y_2	Z_2
.	.	.	.
.	.	.	.
.	.	.	.
.	.	.	.
.	.	.	.
W_n	X_n	Y_m	Z_m
		Highest Score	

Figure 4. Analysis Table Schema for a Particular (e.g., Reading) MLA Sub-Test.

paired list of percentile ranks for these scores. He then performed this same procedure with the CAI group's scores, as schematized in Figure 4. Adams could now answer this question: If a CAI student has a Reading raw score (column 3) that places him at a certain percentile rank in his own class (column 4), at what percentile rank in the control group (column 2) would that same raw score (column 1) have placed him? The Analysis Table in Figure 4 would give the answers for all cases; Figure 3 is a graphic representation of these answers.

3. Thus, in the Reading sub-skill, a CAI student at the 30th percentile of his own class had achieved a raw score that was high enough to place him near the 70th percentile of the control group. In the Writing sub-skill, a student from the CAI group ranked at the 55th percentile of the control class with a raw score that, in his own CAI class, put him no higher than the 20th percentile.

With this much background information on Adams' analytic technique, let us step back and consider what this chart has to say. Again we hear from Adams' "Field Evaluation . . .":

In this plot the CAI students whose scores lie above the diagonal have done better than their counterparts, those whose scores lie below, poorer. An examination of the curves in [Figure 3] shows that for speaking and listening, the two skills *not* [italics added] taught by CAI, the distribution of proficiency in the CAI group was generally similar to that in the reference group. The suggested small deficiency of CAI students in speaking is conceivably related to the fact that they did not use the normal speaking and listening laboratory, hence had little opportunity to practice pronunciation.

No differences in speaking and listening.

By contrast for the skills of reading and writing, the principal skills practiced in the CAI lab, the proficiency distributions are markedly different. In particular, the CAI students in each of the three lowest quartiles scored far higher than their counterparts, so much so that 85 percent of the CAI students did as well or better than the median student in the non-CAI population.

Strong results in reading and writing.

On the basis of questionnaires and other evidence it was determined that the total work time was quite similar for students in the two groups. Thus for these experimental conditions in which the CAI lab was used to provide individualized instruction and remediation, it seems clear that the result was much greater efficiency of learning than was obtained in ordinary group instruction in the university.

CAI produces a greater efficiency of learning.

Adams' discussion of the apparent non-existence of differences between control and experimental groups on the speaking and listening sub-tests is perhaps overly solicitous. The use of a conventional language laboratory was an integral component of the audio-lingual methodology employed at Stony Brook, as is true today of foreign language instruction in general. Naturally, the language laboratory at Stony Brook was used extensively by the control students in the experiment. But the CAI students did not use this language laboratory at all; they used CAI instead. The conventional language laboratory has always been billed as a device addressing itself to the skills of speaking and listening. Thus, there was every reason to expect that the control group performance would significantly surpass the performance of the CAI group in these two skills. But such was not the case. In all likelihood, the Stony Brook laboratory was being utilized at something less than optimal efficiency, and hence failed to contribute to control group learning. In other words, neither CAI nor control students received effective learning experiences in the speaking and listening sub-skills beyond those provided in the classroom during actual student-teacher contact. Hence, neither group would be likely to outperform the other on the MLA sub-tests in Speaking and Listening.

The zero difference in speaking and listening explained.

If this explanation is a sound one, it buttresses the claim that the comparatively large positive effects observed for the Reading and Writing sub-skills can indeed be attributed to the CAI experience. One might suspect, for example, that a special enthusiasm, unpossessed by the control group, existed in or for the CAI class and its teachers because of some positive identification with the CAI equipment or with the ex-

Positive effects substantiated.

perimental setting in general. Thus, any positive experimental effects might be attributable in some way to
this increased level of motivation. But if this were so,
would not one expect to see some sign of positive effect
in all sub-skills tested? As it is, positive effect is observed
just in the Reading and Writing sub-skills, just, in other
words, in skills specifically addressed in the CAI component of the CAI students' course of instruction.

One final point—CAI at Stony Brook monopolized no
more time in the language instruction process than did
the language laboratory. And both were seen as providing secondary support to the primary experience, which
was personal contact with the teacher in the classroom.
The ratios of classroom contact hours to either language
laboratory hours or CAI hours were similar. This fact
is suggestive of a potentially impressive instructional
power inhering in the CAI methodology, for it appears
that the gains attributable to CAI were actually achieved
in relatively small fractions of the students' total instructional time. This suggestion is further enhanced by
the fact that CAI students were exempted from written
homework, it being hypothesized that the CAI laboratory experience would prove a sufficient drill-and-practice
activity.

And so, working with but a fraction of the students'
total instructional time, Adams' CAI conception was able
to generate an effect whereby, at the completion of two
semesters, 80% or more of the CAI group scored higher
than all but 40% of the control group. The effects demonstrated by Adams in this experiment were not merely
significant in a statistical sense, they were large. His
findings, therefore, compelled my respect.

Analysis

Adams' research at IBM is by no means unique in demonstrating the effectiveness of CAI as an instructional
medium. Indeed, there are few who are knowledgeable
in this area of educational technology who would not
accept that well-conceived drill-and-practice CAI can,
given appropriate circumstances of use, be expected to

CAI works, but is too expensive. lead to substantial improvements in instructional quality. In fact, the argument in the literature has passed from one concerning pedagogical efficacy to economic viability of such CAI applications.* And here, perhaps, the success story of drill-and-practice CAI begins to founder, for the performance advantages of CAI, substantial and impressive though they may be in particular instances, would probably not, for a reasonable man, be seen to justify the cost, at least at the present time and for the foreseeable future. As a consequence, and at the present time, "drill-and-practice" CAI is more of a laboratory curiosity than a classroom product, and CAI, as such, is of little immediate practical value.

But, CAI hardware may not be the key factor in CAI success. Although such an assessment may disconcert the manufacturer, to whom CAI is ultimately equated with machinery to be sold, the educator does himself a disservice, I believe, if he makes this same equation, for it is far from obvious that CAI hardware has been the crucial factor in the CAI success stories. After all, much CAI experimentation has failed to produce positive differential results. Obviously, the mere existence of CAI hardware guarantees nothing. Rather, there are good CAI designs and bad ones, just as there are good teachers and bad ones; everything depends on the quality of the learner's experiences as he sits working at the computer terminal. More to the point, it should be kept in mind that the reported findings of CAI experimentation such as Adams' work at Stony Brook are merely effects and might well be achieved in some other modality. Thus, although we may be inclined to place little faith in the near-term future of CAI, it would be a mistake simply to dismiss CAI without first attempting to understand what constitutes good CAI. If we can understand what, in particular, are the causes of effects demonstrated in the Stony Brook study, we may be enabled thereby to discover a way to achieve these effects via a less expensive medium than prohibitively expensive CAI hardware.

* Illustrative is the contribution of D. Jamison, P. Suppes, and C. Butler, "Estimated Costs of Computer Assisted Instruction for Compensatory Education in Urban Areas," *Educational Technology*, Vol. X, No. 9 (September 1970), pp. 49-57.

One cannot be certain why the Stony Brook CAI experiment worked so well; no doubt the full answer is many-sided. I personally believe that a good part of the answer is to be found in the nature of the dialogue that was carried out between a student and the computer, that is to say, in the wisdom of the computer program that controlled the CAI interaction. If one can accept the premise that whatever is learned at all is learned via dialogue with the environment, it becomes an interesting exploration to seek out the differences between the CAI and the control learning environments that might possibly account for the apparent superiority of the CAI experience. Although the truth is no doubt complex, one still does not have far to seek to find prime candidates.

Why did the Stony Brook CAI work so well?

To begin with, consider that throughout this discussion we have been dealing with an area of instruction that can comfortably be said to deal with *skills,* and it is a fact about the acquisition of any skills proficiency that it is facilitated greatly by *practice,* that is, by iterative activity in which a learner successively strives to approximate a performance ideal. What are essential features of effective practice? If practice is to be effective, it must inform the learner, at whatever depth is possible, of the *discrepancies* between his performance and the ideal performance, for the learner himself conceives the challenge to be one of reducing the number and extent of these discrepancies to zero. And also, this information should be presented to the learner when he needs it, that is, while it is still of immediate use to him in the improvement of his ability to perform. Finally, the practice tasks assigned for the learner should take cognizance of the learner's current state of learning relative to a given syllabus or curriculum. It is in precisely these three aspects of practice that the CAI and control learning experiences at Stony Brook were most distinctly divergent.

Skills learning requires extensive supervised practice. CAI provides this.

The CAI computer program used at Stony Brook contained an algorithm (procedure) that, within seconds, corrected a student's performance. For example, imagine that the computer had asked a student to translate a certain English sentence into French:

CAI provided immediate selective correction.

(Computer) The boys will send the book to them.

Had the student typed in the correct answer,

(Student) Les garçons leur enverront le livre.

the computer would have responded affirmatively by typing the letter "c" alongside the student's sentence. Suppose, however, that the student just happened to respond with a sentence that was incorrect in certain particulars, for example:

(Student) Les garçon les enverrons le livre.

Within a few seconds, the computer would return with a message that was, in essence, a reconfiguration of the original practice item, selectively remodeled on the basis of the student's errors.

(Computer) Les garçon– le– – enverron– le livre.

This signal would confirm for the student the extent of his correctness and would indicate specifically where his performance required improvement. At this point, the computer would return control to the student and permit him either to retry the item, this time focusing his attention on his errors, or to request the correct answer, in which case a fully correct answer, with the points of error highlighted, would be presented to the student. Adams coined the term "partial answer feedback" to refer to this type of remediation.

The issue is not that immediate, partial answer feedback has any particular existential greatness. It is not hard to imagine that a professional foreign language teacher could provide selective correction of a greatly superior quality. On the other hand, a state university like Stony Brook cannot approach the student-faculty ratio of Berlitz; indeed, when one compares the quantity of individually supervised practice available to the Stony Brook control group to the practice experiences of the CAI group, one can begin to appreciate the utility of Adams' version of selective correction. Whatever amount of selective correction of errors existed for the control students was performed in the classroom, that is, in a teacher-mediated learning environment, where the extent of immediate personal supervision received by any one student would be directly related to the number of students in the class. Clearly, none of the control students could receive very much individual supervision of his practice. This limitation, which is characteristic of all teacher-mediated classrooms, was probably not mitigated in any significant measure by the homework exercises that the control group were asked to perform, for two reasons. First, whatever correction of errors was actually provided by the class instructors, even when provided the very next day, came at a time when such counsel was no more relevant to students than would be a stop sign that a driver first sees in his rear view mirror after having gone through it. It's yesterday's news. Second, most students cannot realistically be relied upon to check their own mistakes, thereby providing their own selective correction. Thus, the CAI group at Stony Brook received an intensity of individualized selective performance correction that the classroom-based methodology simply could not begin to offer. And immediate selective correction of performance is one of the instructional functions that apparently counts heavily in the acquisition of skills, notably language skills.

Intensity is the key.

Stony Brook CAI, in its essence, provided each CAI student with a "responsive workbook," one that analyzed and appraised his responses as soon as the student wrote them down. But this was not the only major aid to learning provided by IBM's CAI program; the program also provided a *pacing* service to the student. The CAI system kept track of each student's performance and, on the basis of that performance, assigned practice to some that might not be asssigned to others. The system allocated practice differentially, on the basis of a computed estimate of a student's need, the purpose being to maximize the appropriateness of the learning tasks assigned to a student at any particular time.

CAI provided assignments of varying lengths.

The "differential assignment" component of the CAI program worked in roughly the following way:

The entire CAI program was organized into lessons, corresponding to chapters in the textbook that had been assigned for the course. These, in turn, were organized into four or five modules, each module containing ten **The computer** exercise items, e.g., a translation module, a substitution **kept score.** module, etc. As a student proceeded through a module, the system kept a series of scores on his performance, updating a proficiency profile for the module each time the student finished with an item and had generated a score for that item. All students were required by the system to actually perform the first five items of a module. But at the completion of these five items, and after every item in the module subsequently performed, the computer compared various current indices in the proficiency profile with a *sufficiency value* ("escape" threshold) pre-established by the instructor. Whenever the student's proficiency index and the teacher's sufficiency score were equal, the student would be automatically exempted from further work in the module.

The student Thus it might be that a student, upon completion **was released** of the fifth item in the module, would have generated **from a** a high enough proficiency score, and thus be through at **module when** that point. For other students, the exit point might **his score was** come afer the seventh, ninth, or tenth items. Or it might **high enough.** not come until the computer had looped the student back to some previously encountered items. Thus the amount of work assigned to students was variable and depended upon each student's demonstrated performance. One student might do five items; another might do twenty, all in the same module. The net effect was to give more practice to those students whose performance suggested that they could benefit from it.*

IBM's It is no doubt an oversimplification to attribute the **programs** positive results reported in the Stony Brook experiment **should have** exclusively to immediate selective correction and the **worked.**

---

* Details for the assignment algorithm can be found in the article by Adams, Morrison, and Reddy, cited on p. 23. A more sophisticated version of this algorithm, created subsequently for application in Russian language study at the Defense Language Institute, is described in E. N. Adams and P. S. Rosenbaum, *DLI-IBM Joint Feasibility Study in Computer Assisted Foreign Language Instruction,* Final Report, Defense Language Institute. Contract No. DAHC 15-69-C-0145, June 1969.

differential assignment of work. However, these factors should give pause to anyone who would tend to over-emphasize the importance of the computer hardware *per se* in evaluating the Stony Brook results. In all probability, Stony Brook CAI worked less because a machine was involved than because a shrewd learning environment had been designed. IBM's program was based on a sound pedagogical design; it *should* have worked.

It is obviously not without justification that foreign language experts emphasize the importance of small classes. As the ratio of students to teachers becomes smaller, personal classroom dialogue between the individual student and the teacher becomes all the more possible. There is all the more time for the teacher to correct any given student's live performances, down to the ideal limiting case, one teacher for one student. IBM's CAI environment created a one-teacher-on-one-student situation for drill work and practice work such that a student would receive immediate selective correction and individualized work allocation. Certainly the correction that was administered was less sophisticated than what might be presented by a competent teacher, but it vastly exceeded in extent what could be delivered by one teacher to one student in the typical classroom learning situation and, probably for this reason, could achieve its apparently great differential effect. As if to confirm that IBM's CAI program did serve as a surrogate teacher, we may note in Figure 3 that the program affected student's differentially; weaker students got relatively more out of the experience than did stronger students. Again, such a fact should occasion little surprise, for it is the weaker student whom one would expect to benefit most from a treatment that, in a critical aspect of language instruction, could simulate important aspects of effective teacher-student contact.

CAI leads to a net increase in student-teacher contact.

To summarize, CAI is an instrumentality whereby selective correction of errors and differential assignments of work can be achieved on an intensive basis, delivering, with noteworthy effect, instructional assistance to the student in a quantity that no conventionally organized classroom could hope to approach. The only problem is that the instrumentality itself is too costly.

Application of Conclusions

As features of a pedagogy, *immediate selective correction* and *differential assignments* are not foreign concepts to classroom teachers; most exemplars of the teaching profession would see these as being components of good teaching. It is widely accepted that a student cannot in many instances supervise his own work. Left to his own devices, it is thought, the student may not be aware that he has made errors, or he may not know where these errors have occurred, or what they were. Consequently, for this or that reason, the student cannot successfully correct or improve his performance as effectively as can a teacher, and his practice is, therefore, best supervised by a teacher. The problem, to repeat, is not that teachers are unaware of the pedagogical desirability of extensive supervision. It is rather that no matter how assiduously a teacher works at the supervision of classroom activity, conventional group practice techniques are not very efficient: the teacher has just so much real time to interact with individual students, and it is not enough. Of course, the problem is compounded in the extreme in urban settings, where the mandated elementary school class size is typically very large. It is one of the city teacher's greatest frustrations to recognize that such pedagogical necessities as selective correction and differential assignments become mere platitudes when the ratio of students to teachers is large.

But let us note well that the mere fact of large numbers of students is not the primary stumbling block to the implementation of effective supervised practice. The problem resides rather in the vestigial *communications* structure of conventional classrooms. The communica-

tions structure of the typical public school classroom is organized in such a manner as to facilitate, indeed to optimize, the *one-way* transmittal of information. In today's public school instruction, however, actual lecture-presentations are rare occurrences. When they do take place, they are generally short, occupying relatively small segments of the total instructional time. But even though lecture-presentations as classroom events may play a

minuscule role in the overall pattern of today's classrooms in comparison with their historical progenitors,
even so the communications structure that has evolved in
support of this method nonetheless dominates classrooms
even today and renders the execution of effective supervised practice a virtual impossibility, which can readily be
deduced from the schematic in Figure 5. The principal

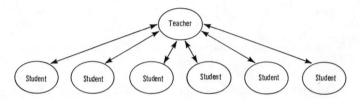

Figure 5. Communications structure of a teacher-mediated learning environment.

limitation in this communications system is that the
teacher cannot carry on a supervisory dialogue with
more than one student at a time. Hence, to the extent
that a teacher is time-shared, the amount of time that any
student may have to interact personally with the teacher
is a function of the number of students in the class, and
in all but the smallest classes, this value becomes dimin-
ishingly small, too small in most instances for even the
highest quality supervision to be effective. One can see
that such a structure is viable only when all students
require the same information at exactly the same time,
as, for example, in orientations and announcements. But,
in a pedagogical situation where varying responses from
students can be expected at varying times, as in many
"individualized" instructional settings, and where these
responses must be acknowledged and responded to appropriately by the teacher within a suitable period of
time, the lecture-presentation structure of classroom
communication is simply too inefficient. A CAI structure guarantees full-time instructional engagement for
each student in the class (see Figure 6).

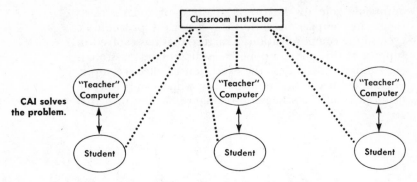

**CAI solves
the problem.**

Figure 6. Communications structure of a CAI learning environment.

The idea! And so arises the question to which the research reported in this book is addressed: Inasmuch as the critical instructional functions in the CAI learning environment are algorithmic, might it not be possible to install a student in the place of the computer and computer terminal and to devise a structured form of interaction that would have this student provide immediate selective correction and differential work assignments for a peer? Historically, this question led directly to the concept of Peer-Mediated Instruction (henceforth designated by the registered trademark PMI®).

CHAPTER 2

The First PMI System

The first embodiment of the Peer-Mediated Instruction concept addressed the subject matter of elementary school *spelling*. This subject matter was selected because it appeared that PMI could offer new and better answers to a series of problems that have plagued spelling systems designers apparently for some time.

Problem: Correction of Errors

Spelling is a skill that requires practice with frequent correction of errors. The most commonly practiced solution to the problem of providing such correction has been a method that relegates correction to checking off wrong items on a test. In spite of the fact that a test is viewed by the student less enthusiastically than practice, and in spite of the fact that posttest correction comes after the fact, this has apparently been the best feasible method of approaching error correction.

Solution:

The assumption underlying PMI is that students themselves can analyze spelling errors and provide effective error correction for each other *even though they themselves may not be sure how to spell the words in question*. A peer-mediated spelling system would call for students to do their work in pairs, one as a "Student,"

39

the other as a "Teacher," the latter providing frequent selective correction for the former, via comparisons the Teacher would make between what the Student writes and what the Teacher sees on the printed page of the text. The frequency of error correction would thus surpass by an order of magnitude the rate of conventional spelling systems.

Problem: Quantity of Practice

Imposing a conventional spelling system on a class of students is a little bit like trying to fit all students into the same size shoe. If every one of those students had a private tutor it would surely be noted that the various tutors would spend different lengths of time and would require differing amounts of practice of their pupils, because of the simple fact that native ability and prior knowledge will differ from student to student. Yet the majority of even the most advanced of the conventional spelling systems impose essentially fixed amounts of work upon all students. In no instance is the amount of practice assigned to students related to an up-to-date assessment of those students' competences. Thus, the majority of students in the class will be getting either more practice than they need, hence will become bored, or too little, hence will experience continual failure, with well-known and very unfortunate emotional consequences.

Solution:

In order to take account of individual differences, PMI would provide a hopefully very simple, very easy-to-learn and use, scoring system that the Teacher in the Student-Teacher pair can use to prescribe variable amounts of practice to his Student depending on a precise estimate that the Teacher makes of how the Student is doing. Thus, every pupil in the class, through the PMI peer interaction, would have assigned to him by his partner *all* of the practice he needs to establish mastery of a block of words, and *just* that amount.

Problem: Tracking

Aural input is a mainstay of any spelling system for the simple reason that the skill finally to be learned is one in which a word shaped in the brain in terms of sound must be rendered in written form. Because it has often been viewed, apparently without any reason beyond convention, that oral presentation of spelling items must be delivered by the classroom teacher, the artificial situation has been created whereby the pace at which students can proceed is no faster or slower than the pace of the classroom teacher. In other words, all students are on the same track, going at the same speed, *regardless of whether they should be going a lot slower or could be going a lot faster.*

Solution:

A PMI system would turn the presentation of oral cues over to the students via a peer-mediated sub-system in which the Teacher dictates spelling items for his Student to practice. Thus, no longer would it be necessary to peg the rate of progress to the pace of the classroom instructor; each Student can proceed at his rate, for his Teacher will present items to be spelled as the Student needs them. Thus, progress is continuous and depends exclusively upon each pupil's demonstrated proficiency.

The foregoing exposition of the advantages claimed for a new spelling system might seem like almost too much of a good thing. If the reader has come this far, however, he can understand the expectations of the research group that was about to begin development of a PMI application in spelling at Teachers College. The system would incorporate three advances in spelling system design. *Any one* of these advances should, it seemed, make possible a better methodology for spelling instruction than had heretofore been available. We thus had reason to hope that the *combination* of these advances would establish the potency of the PMI approach.

What follows is a description of the materials proper,

a description of the pedagogical system by which use was to be made of these materials, and an account of the third grade field trial in which the peer-mediation concept was actualized for the first time.

Materials

The PMI Spelling Kit. The immediate embodiment of the concept was a cardboard box labeled SPELLING, one to be given to each pupil, measuring 9 inches by 11 inches, and the contents thereof. This box was intended to be used by third graders working in pairs. Inside the box were two spirally bound books, one conspicuously labeled Teacher Book, the other, Student Book.

The Teacher Book.

Each page of the Teacher Book contained a spelling lesson of fourteen words. There were eight such lessons (hence eight pages) in the book. Each page had exactly the same format. This format (see Figure 7) was composed of fourteen lines of text. Each line contained one of the words to be mastered in that lesson, followed by a single sentence containing this word, followed by a repeat of the word. Also, at the beginning of each line was a small rectangle (to be used by students in a manner to be discussed).

The Student Book.

The Student Book was nothing more than a special pad that was provided for students functioning as Students to write spelling words on. Each page (see Figure 8) contained a three-column-by-five-row matrix, with each frame subdivided into three sub-rows (serving a purpose to be discussed).

Systems of Use: The Sub-system for Immediate Selective Correction

Each pupil received a box of spelling materials on a permanent basis, but he would use this box just when he was performing as a Student in the peer-mediation

MY NAME IS _____   LESSON **1**
MY BUDDY IS _____   DATE_____

☐ green   Mrs. Turtle wore a green shell.   green

☐ weed   Robert wants to let the weed grow.   weed

☐ teeth   Without teeth, I wouldn't have fun eating.   teeth

☐ meat   I dreamed I ate candy and meat for lunch.   meat

☐ lean   If you lean the other way, you'll fall.   lean

☐ mean   I look mean in my Halloween mask.   mean

☐ she   She sneezed a mighty sneeze.   She

☐ room   Let's find the room with all the toys.   room

☐ spoon   Use your spoon to stir the soda.   spoon

☐ toot   Toot is the only word the train can say.   toot

☐ food   I ate all the food on my plate.   food

☐ true   It's not true that I am a cowboy.   true

☐ blue   Blue rhymes with true.   blue

☐ glue   My glue bottle stuck to my desk.   glue

Figure 7. A page from the Teacher Book for PMI spelling.

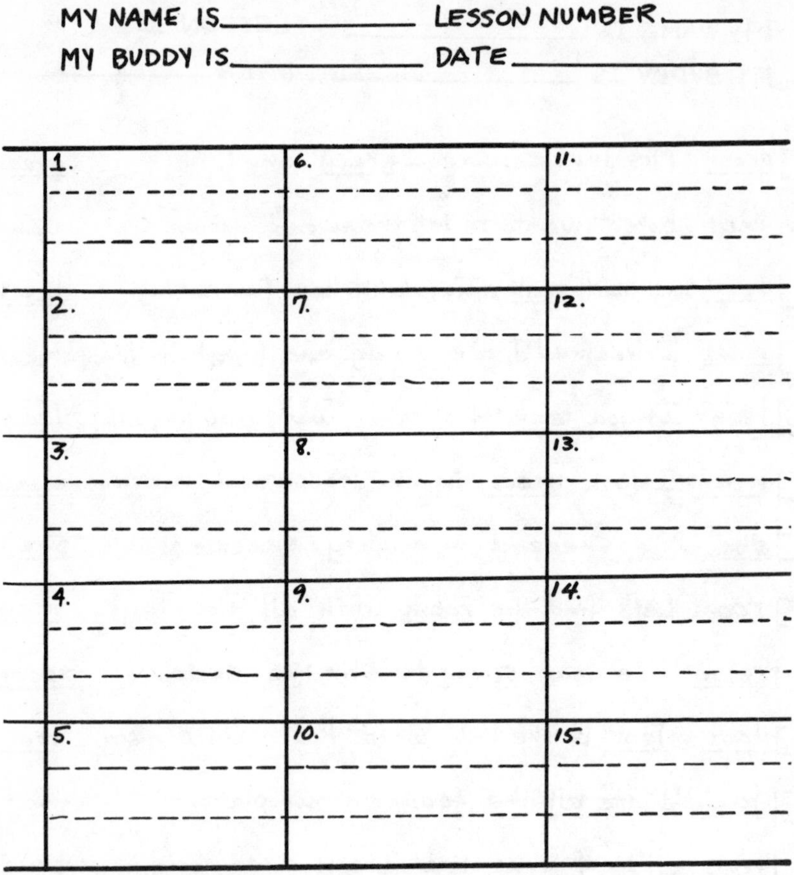

MY NAME IS_____ LESSON NUMBER_____
MY BUDDY IS_____ DATE_____

1.	6.	11.
2.	7.	12.
3.	8.	13.
4.	9.	14.
5.	10.	15.

Figure 8. A page from the Student Book for PMI spelling.

Interactive procedures. dyad. When functioning as a Teacher, therefore, a pupil would be working with the materials of his peer. Thus, at the start of a PMI session, after it had been determined who would be Teacher initially and who would be Student, the Student would take the Student Book out of his box, retain it, and hand his Teacher Book to his

Teacher, who would be seated facing him across a table. The pair would then be ready to begin.

The Teacher would read a target word to the Student, followed by the sentence containing it, followed by a repeat of the word, e.g., from Figure 7, "Green; Mrs. Turtle wore a green shell.; green." The Student would then try to spell the word on the first line of a frame on a Student sheet. After he had spelled the word, the Student would pass his Student Book to his Teacher for correction, or for confirmation of correctness, as the case would be. The Teacher, having completed this task, would then hand the book back to the Student.

This kind of peer interaction lends itself readily to graphical description, as in Figure 9.

It should be recalled at this point that this PMI spelling scheme was conceived as a simulation of a CAI process in which learners are provided with immediate selective correction of errors and differential proficiency-based work assignments. Thus, the correction process itself is one of the two crucial sub-systems of the spelling scheme. In giving structure to the former, special regard had to be given to the special subject matter characteristics of spelling and to the viability of various correction procedures for young children.

The learning task that most closely approximates the actual skill of spelling is the writing out of words on the basis of some stimuli (e.g., a spoken word, a written synonyn, etc.) other than the written version of the word itself, which would simply be copying. Such a task is *complex,* in the sense that the learner's response contains many different sequentially ordered elements, i.e., the letters of the word. In such circumstances, it would be of limited effectiveness to correct the student's performance simply by indicating that it is right or wrong. This would be the equivalent of a computer saying to the programer, "There's a bug in your program." But where? The computer's message would give the programer no information on how to fix up the program. By the same token the one bit of information offered to the student who misspelled a word would give that student zero information on *how* to improve his performance,

The necessity of selective correction in spelling.

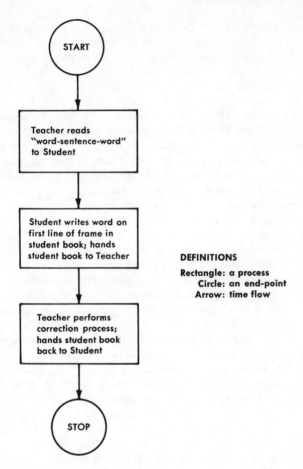

Figure 9. Flowchart Summary I: The Correction Process.

no information on how the performance of the student departs from the ideal. And so it is natural to search for a richer form of correction, one that would provide more information content than simply the one bit implicit in "Right" or "Wrong."

One can imagine a quite complex form of correction that takes into account the three ways (and their com-

binations) in which the spelling of a word may be de-
formed: the omission of letters, the substitution of incorrect letters for correct ones, and the addition of
extraneous letters. In the early phases of our experi-   **Trade-offs.**
mentation, however, we discovered an important trade-
off between the richness of the correction system and
the sheer viability of the communication mechanics
through which the correction sub-system is implemented.
In particular, we noted two unfortunate concomitants of
such increased richness. First, the richer the system of
correction became, the more likely it would be that
Teachers would make errors in performing the correction process. Secondly, the increased complexity would,
by making great demands on the Teacher, result in slow-
ing down the rate of interaction to a point exceeding
satisfactory limits. If the pace of interaction slowed griev-
ously, the interaction would simply collapse, with the
Student no longer paying attention .

(It is an interesting sidelight that students sitting at
CAI terminals display variable patience limits waiting
for responses from the machine. Importantly, these limits
are apparently activity-dependent; that is, the limits
vary with different kinds of CAI activities. For example,
a child doing an arithmetic drill, e.g., $7 + 14 = ?$,   **Variable**
will demand a much faster response from the system than   **patience in**
will the student who has just spent thirty seconds enter- **waiting for**
ing the translation of a sentence from English to Russian. **response.**
This seems to have something to do with the degree of
complexity assumed for the task by the student.)

After much trial-and-error experimentation, we
reached a compromise on the correction system, one
richer than a one bit system, but one that could be
executed accurately and rapidly by students. This system
has the Teacher compare the word that a Student has
written with the correct spelling (in the Teacher Book)
according to the following procedures:

The Teacher does a character-by-character match between the Student's response and the correct spelling in
the Teacher Book, the first characters in each word, the
seconds, the thirds, and so forth. If the Teacher comes
to a mismatch, he draws a line vertically through the

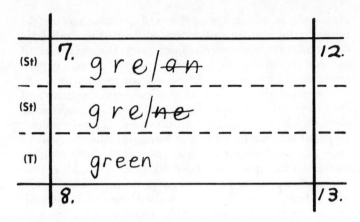

Figure 10. A Student Book frame.

Student's word at that point and then puts a horizontal line through the rest of his word. Thus, if the Student has misspelled the word "spoon,"

spune

the Teacher would overwrite this spelling as follows:

sp |une

The com-
promise.   If "green" had been misspelled,

grean

then as follows

gre |an

In any particular instance, the message to the Student is clear. For instance, in gre |an, it says, "Everything you have written to the left of the vertical slash is correct, but somewhere to the right of that slash there is an error." And so, in this manner, one pupil can provide immediate selective correction for another, very nearly simulating IBM's computer-generated "partial answer feedback" in the process.

On any particular item, a Student was permitted two tries in succession before being required to move on to the next word. The interaction worked like this:

If the student had spelled the word correctly on his first try, the Teacher would simply confirm the success and go on to the next word. If the word was spelled incorrectly, the Teacher would provide partial answer correction and have the Student try the word again.

If again the word was spelled incorrectly, the Teacher would correct the Student's response, but would this time also write the correct spelling for the Student to see on the third line of the frame.

Thus, as in the following simulation:

Teacher reads out loud: Green; Grass is green; green.

Student writes: *grean*

Teacher overwrites: *gre/an*

Student writes: *grene*

Teacher overwrites: *gre/ne*

Teacher writes: *green*

This dialogue represents a transduction of the Student Book frame in Figure 10.

Below, in Figure 11, we update the graphics.

Systems of Use: The Sub-system for Differential Work Assignments

The Teacher operates a second sub-system, one whose purpose is to assign differential amounts of practice to the Student in accordance with the apparent state of the Student's proficiency. It works as follows:

Whenever the Student gets a word correct on the top line of a frame, the Teacher places a check in the rectangular box provided alongside that word in the Teacher Book. *Only on this occasion* is this box used;

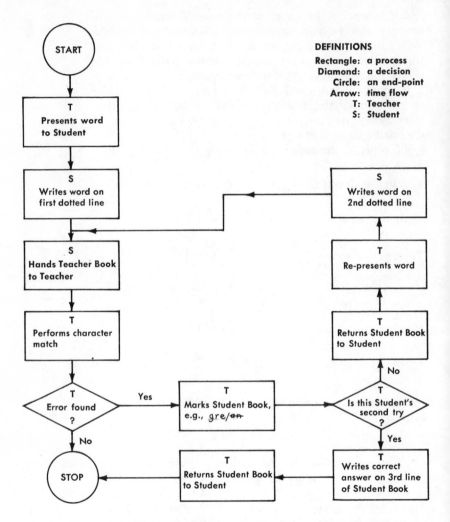

Figure 11. Flowchart Summary II: The Correction Process.

if a Student gets the word wrong on the first line of the frame, but gets it right on the second line, when the word is re-presented, even so the Teacher does not check off the box. Thus it will likely be that after the Teacher takes the Student through a full page of spelling words, some of the boxes will have been checked, others not, in particular those that the Student has spelled incorrectly.

The crux of the supervisory algorithm is this: At the end of a "pass," that is, having administered the full list of eligible words, the Teacher inspects the page that has just been completed. If there still remain any boxes that have *not* been checked off, the Teacher initiates a new cycle. He first asks the Student to turn to a clean page in the Student Book. He then starts re-presenting the words in the list, but this time *just those words for which the associated box has not yet been checked off,* just those, in other words, that the Student has not demonstrated his ability to spell on the preceding cycle.

Presenting to the Student just the unchecked words, the Teacher proceeds through the list, checking off each word that the Student this time spells correctly on the first try. When it has been completed, the Teacher again inspects the Teacher Book page. If there are still unchecked words, the Teacher initiates yet another cycle, and another, and another, until all of the words have finally been checked off, that is, until the Student has spelled all the words correctly on some first effort. This is presented graphically in Figure 12.

Thus, through the execution of this scoring algorithm, the student Teacher, automatically and without having to think about it at all, assigns differential amounts of practice to his peer.

In other words, we have now a paper and pencil simulation of what was certainly one of the most productive CAI drill-and-practice programs ever devised. The complete interaction is graphically described in Figure 13.

The Field Trial

In planning the first field trial, first and foremost in our minds, beyond all other things, was the question of whether our peer-mediation scheme could work as a system of classroom operations. For months prior to actual use of a prototype in a classroom, in anticipation of a variety of contingencies, we spent much time debugging various pieces of the system in short laboratory-like experiments with pairs of students "borrowed" **Debugging** from their regular classes. During these days the basic **and system** mechanics of peer-mediation were developed *and* studied. **design** **modifications.** Dozens of questions were asked, such as: (1) How intricate

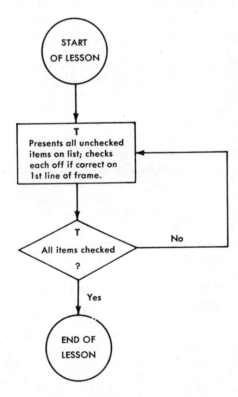

Figure 12. Flowchart Summary III: The Differential Assignment Procedure.

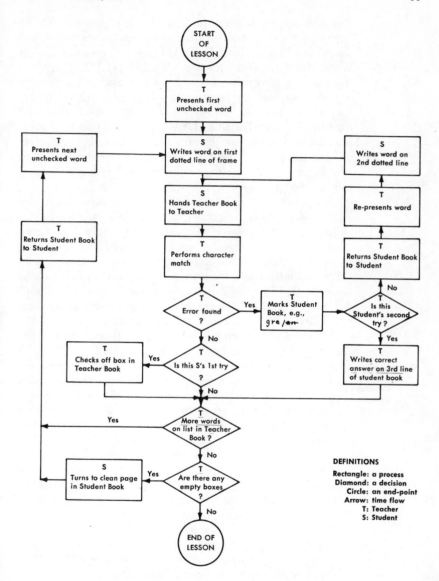

Figure 13. Complete pedagogy of Peer-Mediated Instruction
system for spelling in the P. S. 129 field trial.

can the scoring algorithm be at various grade levels or ages? (2) How many continuous attempts at an individual item should be allowed? (3) What kinds of remediation algorithms are feasible, are optimal? (4) What are the parameters governing attention span, and what are the optimal values? (5) How wide ought to be the desk between the two buddies? (6) What are the factors involved in the rate of interaction? (7) What are the effects of peer-mediated instruction on the interpersonal encounter? These and many other aspects of detail were examined in the hope that the system would ultimately meet the acid test of actual classroom use.

Right up to the start of the first classroom test, we had considerable uncertainty about the ultimate viability of peer-mediated instruction; not only did it contain some fairly novel classroom procedures, but also, we could only guess about certain basic components of peer mediation as a *classroom* (as opposed to *laboratory*) system: (1) How should classroom teachers be orientated? (2) How should these teachers give orientation to their students? (3) How should pairing be accomplished?

The spelling scheme was given a field trial during the New York Public School summer session of 1970 under the auspices of P.S. 129 in Manhattan. The project involved two classes of third graders, each starting out with approximately 20 students. This trial did not involve a comparative study; no attempt was made to prove that peer-mediated spelling instruction works better than garden-variety spelling instruction. Rather, the trial had more in common with the first test flight of a new aircraft. Simulation testing tells just so much about how an aircraft will perform under actual flight conditions; the real question, or certainly the ultimate question, is what will happen when an attempt is made to fly the plane. Obviously, too, a severe design miscalculation in any sensitive sub-system would result in a failure, total or partial, of the system as a whole. The P.S. 129 spelling project represented the inevitable next step, one that was esssential to round out our understanding of the peer-mediation sub-systems, in particular such sub-systems as

P.S. 129 as a learning experience for systems designers.

could only be studied in a live instructional setting. Here is what we learned from the trial run of the PMI spelling prototype at P.S. 129.

Instructor Orientation

The P.S. 129 field experience showed us that, far and away, a good understanding of exactly how the system should work in the classroom is a sufficient end product for instructor orientation. Although there is no doubt that a detailed description and explanation of PMI concepts, materials, and procedures, followed by a "hands-on" simulation by instructors of Teacher and Student roles, followed, finally, by a review to ensure mastery, would constitute a highly effective instructor orientation program, any form of orientation that accomplishes the first-mentioned end will suffice.

The instructor needs only to understand the system.

Pupil Orientation

In planning the field trial, we had been grappling with the question of whether to impose a pupil orientation procedure upon our cooperating teachers, one reflecting how *we* at Teachers College thought an orientation for pupils might best be performed, or to leave the teachers free to exercise their own judgment. We chose the latter, on two grounds: First, we found that we could not ourselves agree in sufficient detail on either the philosophy, the psychology, or the pedagogy of the orientation. Second, we noted that if we used an orientation of our own, then, quite aside from the question of whether it would work, we would have no way to know whether any perhaps quite different approaches to orientation might be viable. And so, we asked of our two cooperating teachers simply that they use their discretion in conducting an orientation for their students; they should do it in their own way.

Instructor's choice.

Our decision, as it turned out, was a fortunate one, for indeed, our teachers went about orientation in quite different ways. We witnessed two such and called them the *hands-off* and *hands-on* approaches.

In the orientation we characterized as hands-off, the

Two modes of orientation emerged.

teacher kept the students at their desks, facing front, with their materials available, and explained the system. Only upon completion of this teacher-centered presentation, which took the better part of two half-hour periods, were the students permitted to open their materials and get to work. The students were then paired off and the first actual practice using Peer-Mediated Instruction was allowed to begin.

Hands-off!

In the *hands-on* approach, pupils were paired off and asked to work with the materials almost from the outset. They were given a bare minimum of instruction by the classroom teacher, who spent most of his time walking from pair to pair, monitoring each, making occasional remarks to the class as a whole, and, in general, "picking up the pieces" and "sorting out loose ends."

Hands-on!

Those readers with classroom experience may well consider one of these approaches to be better *a priori* than the other, as indeed I did at the time. When, during the first session, it was noted by an observer that one of the teachers was not going to permit his pupils to open up their materials, I was interested, for I was taken at the time, as I still am, with the notion that students learn to do what they *do* when they learn. For on so many occasions I had witnessed the non-transferability of a learned skill from one modality to another. I reasoned, accordingly, that the *hands-off* approach would fail, or if not fail, then at least seriously retard the pupils in learning PMI procedures.

A prediction that failed.

As it turned out, my prognostication was quite wrong, for at the end of the third session (1½ hours), the pupils in the *hands-off* class were performing PMI procedures with as much facility as the second class, which had a *hands-on* orientation; in fact, with no noteworthy exceptions, both classes were carrying out PMI rather well. By the end of that third session, the instructors and the team from Teachers College could all agree that the students had learned the system and could make it work. Now, in retrospect, it it not all that amazing that the hands-off approach worked as well as it did, for, indeed, neither teacher employed a *pure* strategy. The hands-off

Both strategies can work.

approach did have a significant measure of hands-on, and conversely. What we learned, therefore, is simply that the proportions of mix between hands-off and hands-on are not critical within extremely broad limits, a salutary operating characteristic of PMI that all but eliminates the pedagogical structure of a PMI student orientation as a problematic aspect of successful PMI implementation. Teachers could apparently make the system work with no difficulty.

Pairing

During the laboratory phases of our development work, we had ample opportunity to observe how psychological factors could affect peer mediation as a communications system. We noticed two effects that ultimately were to play a key role in working out the procedures for pairing students that we asked the classroom instructors to follow.

Firstly, to any instructional engineer, the basic human factor in working with learners is variance in ability; not necessarily ability as tested, but ability as observed in relation to the tasks the learner is being asked to perform. The definitions of "weakly" and "strongly" able emerge along two correlated dimensions. "Weak" students are those who do poorly on tests *and* those who execute procedures slowly, and conversely for the "strong" students. During the laboratory phase of our research, we observed a pattern that hindered effective interaction whenever we paired a very weak learner and a very strong learner. There are, not surprisingly, critical limits to the difference between two students in their ability to execute procedures. When these limits are exceeded, it is as if the learners are suddenly speaking two different languages, with neither being able to get his own needs satisfied or to satisfy his own demands or those of his partner, this often leading to a breakdown of the dyadic relationship.

Effects of ability differences.

Consequently, we arrived at the operational principle that if the selection pool from which pairs are drawn contains learners who are extremely divergent in ability, the pool should initially be subdivided according to ability.

Sub-grouping may sometimes be necessary.

The absolute
necessity for
random,
sessional
pairing.

Secondly, PMI is an interpersonal encounter. Even though there are rules of the game, these rules are not visible for the player. These rules serve only to give structure to interpersonal encounter. Not surprisingly, unfortunate interpersonal factors can occasionally dominate the instructional system proper to the extent of causing changes in the latter beyond the point of effectiveness. In short, for optimal effectiveness, it is advisable to establish pairing as a daily or a sessional event, with new partners selected for each session. Thus, the antagonisms that might arise in a locked and inescapable encounter simply do not arise. If any student perceives his relationship with his peer to be a bad one, he can also accept his state as temporary, a state that will be different during the next PMI session. Better still if there is a *random* element in the pairing process. For then, a pupil's current state of pairing will be perceived by him not only as temporary, but as an act of God.

In the P.S. 129 study, the *randomization* system was not particularly well designed, and had to be scrapped. The teacher made assignments on a discretionary basis, trying to randomize the pairing as much as possible. But the *sessional* aspect of the pairing was preserved, and it served well.

Subsequent field studies of PMI systems have all attested to the utility, indeed necessity, of the principle of *random, sessional pairing*.

System Performance

On the first day of the trial, before the commencement of the student orientation to the PMI spelling system, all of the students were given a pretest (dictation format) based upon 45 words randomly selected from the 120-word course syllabus. As a student would finish the course (in particular, during the next class session devoted to spelling), a 45-word posttest was administered to that student. Four alternate forms of the posttest were constructed and used; for each, care was taken to ensure an equal sampling from each of the eight lessons in the course. The extent of spelling achievement for the

Percentage
Score

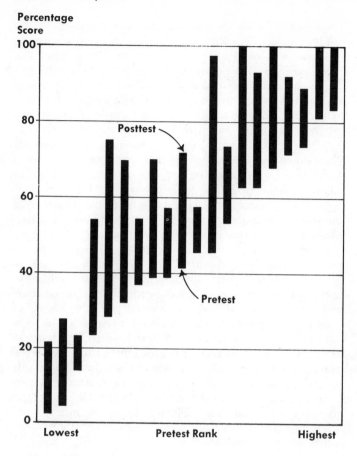

Figure 14. Pre-Post comparison on 20 survivors in PMI spelling.

20 students who both started *and* completed the spelling
program is reflected in Figure 14.

It is evident merely from inspection that significant
learning gains resulted from the PMI spelling experience,
in fact, an average increase in spelling proficiency of 24
percentage points, from a pretest mean of 45% to a
posttest mean of 69%. (This pre-post difference could
probably have been larger were it not for the ceiling

Students did learn.

effect observed for the upper tercile of the group; i.e., no student could do better than get all the words correct.)

Thus, we could now know that peer-mediation can have positive instructional effect. What we could not know, however, was how the PMI methodology stacks up against more conventional methodologies that might also claim positive effect. As noted earlier, no attempt was made to phase a comparative evaluation into the P.S. 129 field trial. The trial was intended as a check-out (or shakedown) of the PMI system functions, not as a procedure for ascertaining output characteristics relative to other instructional methodologies.

But how much learning is a lot?

Still, it is possible to make a comparison with an *ideal* reference methodology, that is, an hypothesized methodology that acquires its credibility as a function of how closely this idealization approximates classroom procedures for teaching spelling. It is not a difficult task to project an ideal control methodology if we are willing to accept on faith that the directions for use that accompany published materials of instruction, in the form of "teacher's editions," bear reasonable relation to conventional practices. Although I have no direct evidence to support this conjuncture, it is apparently widely believed among elementary school teachers that their peers rely greatly on these manuals and that for spelling, in particular, lessons are conducted in close accordance at least to the major guidelines offered. Thus, we might infer from the materials themselves something about conventional classroom practice.

A comparison can be made with an idealized version of conventional methodology.

An approximation of conventional practice.

Most elementary school spelling textbooks are arranged in 36 sequential weekly lessons (including 6 review lessons). Not uncommonly at the third grade level, three to five half-hour sessions will be devoted to spelling each week, covering in this manner one lesson a week for 36 weeks. Also, at the third grade level, a lesson will introduce roughly 15 words in each lesson. Suffice just these premises about conventional public school spelling instruction.

Now, an interesting question emerges that has to do with the extent to which new words actually are new. The layman, thumbing through a child's spelling test, would probably automatically assume that the 15 words in the word list for an arbitrary lesson are all new words, that is, words that the students do not know and are going to learn in the process of covering the lesson. Not only is this assumption untrue, but its truth would imply certain absurd pedagogical consequences. One of the teacher's highest responsibilities is to make sure that the materials students are working with are not too hard for them. Thus, a teacher will strenuously avoid assigning blocks of material that are totally new to all of the students in the class, for here how could the teacher possibly know whether the material is just right or much too advanced? So, in fact, when students are programed as a group to a particular syllabus, in our case to a selection of spelling words, some of the students are going to know some of the words.

Students always know some of the new material.

This fact has interesting ramifications, particularly as one begins to speculate on the average level of pre-knowledge existing in the conventional spelling classroom. The class of P.S. 129 can serve as one reference point (see Figure 14). Here the median value is 42%. The least knowledgeable student in the class knew 1 of the 45 words on the pretest; the most knowledgeable knew 37.

At any value greater than zero, the pre-knowledge value has significance for determining the efficiency of the conventional methodology; for the existence of pre-knowledge means that the number of words that could *in principle and fact* be learned in whatever period of time is devoted by the class to a lesson is limited by the number of words in the lesson that are *not already known*. If a student knows 2 of 15 words, he can learn 13 words by studying the lesson; if he knows 12 words, however, he can only learn 3. (Here, one can observe one of the cardinal deficiencies of "lock-step" methodologies; the more a student knows, the more is his freedom to learn curtailed.) Thus, we now have a means of comparing the potential of PMI spelling against conventional spelling, for the number of words actually learned by the PMI students can be divided by the number of hours spent on the course to derive for each the number

A student can't learn words he already knows.

Rates of acquisition can be compared.

of words actually learned on average in a single PMI hour. This figure can then be compared with the number of words that could be new, and hence learnable *at all*, under a conventional methodology.

The extent of pre-knowledge for the P.S. 129 third grade was 45%, meaning that the average student knew roughly seven words and thus, in the time allotted in one week of instruction to the lesson under a conventional methodology, *could* learn roughly eight words. In fact, under the PMI system, the average student, in 1½ hours of instruction, *did* learn roughly 14 words, an increment in learning system output of 75%. But even this figure is overly generous to the conventional methodology, for it assumes that the effectiveness of the method itself is 100%, that is, that every student will learn every word he does not know during the time allotted under the method. But this assumption cannot be sustained in practice; the mere fact that a student studies a word obviously in no way implies that he will learn it during the studying time. No method is going to teach all children all the material they do not know; the question to be asked of the conventional methodology is not one of the *existence* of inefficiency, but one of *extent*. Just how much of what the student did not know before does he come away knowing after exposure to the typical spelling treatment? Table 1 permits the reader to contrast PMI

PMI's superiority ranges from the convincing to the compelling.

Table 1. Projected superiority in efficiency of PMI as a function of actual efficiency of conventional methodology, assuming 1½ hours of spelling instruction per week (based on an average of 29 words learned in an average time of 3.3 PMI class hours).

Percentage Efficiency of Conventional Methodology	Percentage Incremental Superiority of PMI over Conventional Methodology
100%	75%
75	133
50	250
25	600
0	∞

and conventional methodology at several values of in-efficiency.

The only question remaining is to inquire into the actual extent of inefficiency in conventional spelling practice. In general, I would not expect the efficiency rating to be very high at all, probably not above 50%.

And so, PMI would appear to fare well in comparison with a hypothetical but probably representative reference population. Indeed, if similar results were obtained in an actual contrastive study, they would be considered definitive. In fact, a teacher would feel compelled to consider using the new methodology, all other things being equal.

Roles and Learning

The P.S. 129 field trial provided one new dimension of understanding that had a particularly great impact on me personally. While still at IBM, when the possibilities of Peer-Mediated Instruction were just suggesting themselves, I inevitably, by association with CAI, viewed the entire PMI interaction in terms of a man-machine dyad. I thought of the peer Teacher as exercising functions of the computer. I was even prepared to let a student spend half of his time as a "computer," possibly learning nothing, for this could be justified in terms of the enormously powerful experience that this same student would have as a Student. In the course of the P.S. 129 field trial I discovered the narrowness of the CAI metaphor.

The CAI metaphor is too narrow.

The terms Student and Teacher, which are used throughout this book to describe peer-mediating roles, are misleading in one aspect of their semantics. They suggest that one member of the pair, the one doing the Teaching, is not doing any learning, which is emphatically not true. Everyone who was involved in systematic observation of the PMI field trial commented to the effect that being a Teacher was quite possibly as contributory a learning experience for the student as was being a Student. As of this writing, no systematic studies have been carried out on the extent of learning that takes

Pupils learn both as Students and as Teachers.

place for a PMI Teacher. Still, I do not think it would be in error to assert that Teacher and Student are labels that have merely procedural significance and that the structured activities in which both peers are engaged can lead to learning for both, provided both the Teacher's procedures and the Student's procedures address the subject matter in an appropriate fashion.

PMI and Discipline

An observer can tell when learning is taking place in a classroom, or at the very least when the attention of students is engaged, simply by noticing how many pairs of eyes are drawn by one's appearance as a stranger in the classroom. PMI systems can apparently score high on this test, probably for the simple reason that the attention of PMI students is occupied all the time. Quite aside from the purely pedagogical significance of this feature of operation, one should be aware of a predictable consequence for an important dimension of the social life of the classroom, namely, discipline, and in particular the disciplinary problems that arise from a state of boredom. The frequency of such problems should diminish to near zero, a prediction that the P.S. 129, and all subsequent, PMI experiences, have strongly confirmed.

Discipline problems tend to disappear.

Concluding Remark

The P.S. 129 field trial was encouraging. The positive learning gains tended to confirm the validity of the pedagogical principles underlying Peer-Mediated Instruction. These results justified the expectation that these principles would be as effective as a paper-and-pencil modality as they had been in a computer-based modality. Quite aside from buttressing the soundness of PMI pedagogy, the field trial left us with the impression that we had reached adequate solutions to the engineering problems associated with implementing PMI concepts as a workable classroom system. This is not to say that we did not learn a great deal from the experience that would enable us to build a better system the next time, but rather that our doubts concerning the ultimate classroom viability were dispelled. And so, the way lay open to attack the next order of challenge—the broadening of PMI from a "special purpose" plan of instruction to an operational "general purpose" system, one capable of accommodating a broader range of instructional objectives and arbitrarily selected instructional materials.

CHAPTER 3

From Special to General Purpose

The experimental application of the PMI concept at P.S. 129 showed that the basic interactional mechanics of IBM's drill-and-practice CAI concept could indeed be simulated within the domain of a paper-pencil-print technology. In terms of the overall goal—the development of a general purpose instructional control system— the P.S. 129 experience was but a step along the way. But it was a critical step, for had it so turned out that, for some irreconcilable cause, the peer-mediation interaction could not be contained in the classroom, then this entire approach to instructional control most likely would have had to be scrapped. As it happened, the system proved itself to be particularly efficacious.

Still, the system innovated at P.S. 129 was a special purpose system in that the 120 words presented in the Teacher Book defined and totally circumscribed the content and behavioral objectives that could be addressed by that particular system. There is nothing especially wrong or morally suspect about a special purpose instructional control system, particularly if it can be packaged as a text and marketed at a price competitive with conventional texts. After all, such an eventuality would almost without question result in a subject matter specific improvement in classroom productivity. (Holt, Rinehart and Winston, Inc., is currently producing an elementary school spelling program with the PMI concept as the basis for instructional management.) If the benefits of improved instructional control are to be derived in the near future, however, a general purpose approach is called for, in particular an approach that will make it possible for school personnel to program for use under a good instructional control system either home-made instructional materials or off-the-shelf instructional materials that, when published, were intended for use under conventional methods.

The initial approach to a general purpose PMI system was less a matter of plan than of circumstances of patronage. Specifically, the conversion of PMI, the special purpose system, to a system henceforth to be called PMI/MS,* the general purpose version, was supported financially by the American Telephone & Telegraph Company, in particular by its Department of Environmental Affairs, who recognized the possibility that PMI/MS could establish itself as a viable system of instructional control in remedial training environments of the Bell System. Specifically, AT&T hoped that Teachers College could create an operations manual that could be disseminated throughout the Bell companies and used by those companies either to implement PMI/MS or to make use of various features of the system to improve currently existing methods. It is the supremest irony that the form of packaging for PMI/MS dictated by the circumstances of the AT&T work was a manual, i.e., a book, precisely the medium that prompted Thorndike to comment in the first place on the desirability of an improved instructional control technology. And indeed, for exactly the same reasons as those expressed by Thorndike in his prescient discussion, the biggest single question mark in the future of PMI/MS as a general purpose system seemed at the time to reside in whether the book form of presentation, certainly the cheapest medium

Enter AT&T and the concept of a PMI Manual.

---

* Peer-Mediated Instruction/Management System.

for delivering PMI/MS, could provide a viable interface between the system as a product and the institutional user.

Bases of a Collaboration

AT&T evolved an interest in developing the PMI concept against a background of numerous perceived deficiencies in industrial remedial training, to wit:

Problems in remedial training in industry.

1. Little consistency in either instructional content or approach.
2. Weak and often inconclusive rationales for particular syllabi or methodologies.
3. Unimpressive reported instructional gains.
4. Virtually non-existing cost-benefit accounting.
5. Wide variation in teacher competence.

Possible advantages of PMI.

Against this panoply, peer mediation could well appear to stand out as an attractive alternative. Beginning with the last point first, a PMI system is one whose successful operation does not entail systematic intervention or mediation by the classroom teacher; the system is operated and maintained by the students themselves. Students control themselves and each other. The consequence is a favorable one, in which the output of the learning environment overall is seen to become considerably less correlated with variability in teaching competence. Thus, **Little need for instructor intervention.** the need for highly trained teaching talent becomes, at least for skills instruction, less important. Under a PMI system, what is called for from the instructor is less subject matter expertise than management ability to service the needs of students who are going about the business of learning on their own. In short, PMI systems promise a substantial increase in the thriftiness with which teaching resources are used. The concept of "good teaching" implies the existence of ideal mediational forms; a teacher can only be a "good" teacher relative to some methodology. Relative to PMI, a greater percentage of teachers should prove to be competent, i.e., "good," teachers.

A second factor of interest to AT&T was that PMI, being a pedagogy, exhibits relative independence from course content. Thus, even though different texts might be in use throughout the Bell System for remedial training purposes, there was the possibility that a PMI system could accommodate all such materials in current use. On the question of which learning materials are to be used in particular instances, schools are as parochial as law or custom will allow; getting different concerned parties to agree on which materials are best in particular instances is often a near impossibility. Autonomy in materials selection is zealously guarded by the schools. What PMI says to the teacher or the curriculum planner, however, is this: Use any materials at all, but organize classroom activity relating to these materials in a manner conforming to the activity patterns of Peer-Mediated Instruction. And so, the AT&T sponsor could reasonably hope that PMI would not only prove viable in a particular Bell System environment, but could, without much travail, be transported to and be used with success in other environments, ensuring in the process an increased measure of instructional consistency, *even granting the use of different materials of instruction.*

Adaptability of PMI to existing materials.

A third factor: In a PMI system, the environment conforms to the rhythm of the student, and not vice versa, as is the case in "lock-step" environments. Quite aside from the large positive emotional and attitudinal effects that this can have on the learner toward the system, a PMI system permits a technique of cost control of greatly increased sensitivity. In a conventional "lock-step" instructional methodology, instructional time is paid for each student regardless of whether need for that time is indicated by the student's performance. Furthermore, in a conventional system, instruction is halted at the end of a certain period of time regardless of whether the student has learned all that he is capable of learning. In short, a lock-step methodology can, in principle, provide too much instructional time or too little, and, in practice, inevitably will. A well-conceived PMI system provides each student with whatever learning time that student requires, and, hence, provides school administration

Unlocking the lockstep permits improved cost control.

with a way of directly relating cost (i.e., time) to performance. That this is a desirable, even necessary, feature of any system of instructional cost accountability should go without saying.

Finally, PMI, on the face of its prior performance both as a CAI and as a paper-and-pencil technology, could be seen as a potentially powerful instructional technique, one that could lead directly to impressive gains in instructional output.

On the strength of such considerations as these, the Department of Environmental Affairs at AT&T proposed an interesting collaboration, one that would provide AT&T with a medium of delivery whereby **The purposes** PMI/MS could be applied widely to remedial skills **of the** training in reading in the Bell System and in urban **collaboration.** high schools, and with a quantitative comparison of PMI/MS performance against the performance of a currently used conventional instructional methodology. For the research contingent from Teachers College, the collaboration would yield observations and measurements that would definitively corroborate or disconfirm the principles upon which Peer-Mediated Instruction is based and a verdict on the real-world viability and utility of a fully implemented peer-mediated instructional control system, an assessment, in other words, of the benefits that can be anticipated when a *teacher-mediated* learning environment is converted into a *peer-mediated* learning environment.

In its essence, the collaboration called for two activities: First, a peer-mediated instructional control system was to be designed and mediated in the form of a **TC designs a** Manual that could be used by Bell System training spe- **Manual and** cialists in the creation, implementation, and management **tests it.** of their own version of PMI/MS (based upon materials and objectives of their own choosing). Second, a version of PMI/MS was actually to be created and implemented in strict accordance with the Manual, thus making it possible at the same time to explore the feasibility and efficacy of PMI/MS in general and to revise and perfect the Manual as operational experience might dictate.

Notes on the Creation of the Manual

Note 1

In the back of this book, beginning on page 165, is a document that henceforth will be referred to as the PMI/MS Manual, or, simply, the Manual. The most important point to make initially is that it is *not merely a description* of a general purpose system of Peer-Mediated Instruction, but a *functioning component* of that system. The Manual interfaces the PMI instructional system with the environment (i.e., the larger system) in which the PMI system is to be brought into existence. It is the Manual to which an interested party turns for an image of what PMI/MS will look like once it has been implemented. It is the Manual to which the classroom instructor's attention is directed during his period of orientation to the management responsibilities associated with the classroom operation of PMI/MS. And it is the Manual to which reference is made for the maintenance of successful PMI/MS operations. Thus it is, that if the Manual is sufficiently deficient in its description in any crucial particular of the system, the system could not work; hence, the importance of the Manual.

The Manual is part of the system as well as being the system.

Note 2

In sharp contrast with the instructional "system" that can be inferred from the typical Teacher's Edition of a conventional textbook series in the language skills, PMI/MS exhibits considerable sophistication and complexity. Indeed, PMI/MS confronts the potential user with a new and unfamiliar terrain. But it is the newness of the terrain that may come as something of a surprise, and not the fact that crossing it presents any particular difficulty. The reader will, furthermore, receive his first exposure to this terrain through the "keyhole" that is provided by the Manual. And so, the design of the Manual called for meticulous care to be paid to the communicational characteristics of the Manual so that it might as effectively as possible bridge the gap between

PMI is a new kind of terrain.

conventional assumptions and the concepts of Peer-Mediated Instruction.

The problem boiled down to one of describing a system (in the sense of a set of *cooperating* parts) through the medium of academic prose style, as it is in particular typified by such handbooks of English as the *Macmillan Handbook of English*:*

The parts of the outline, heads and subheads, should be labeled by alternating figures and letters as follows: I, II, III, and so on; A, B,C, and so on; 1, 2, 3, and so on; a, b, c, and so on.

Graphically, we observe that such a writing structure imposes a *tree-like* organization on content (Figure 15). The particular problem that arises is that a tree structure does not allow *overlap*. For example, there is no way in which the sub-tree I-A-1 could possibly overlap the sub-tree II-B-2. In and of itself, this fact about trees is of no special importance. But consider that we are not talking about anything so mathematically simple as categorizations or taxonomies; we are talking about *systems*. In *Of a Fire On the Moon*, hear Norman Mailer on systems in Apollo 11:

Each system was designed with parallel and complementary functions, the equivalent of a network of roads between any two cities. A variety of routes existed wherever it was desired to shift some system in Apollo 11 from one condition to another, just as one always has the choice of superhighways, highways, country roads, feeder roads, and in emergency, simple dirt lanes in transit from one place to another.

PMI/MS is not a tree; it is a semi-lattice.

PMI/MS, along with the space flight system of Mailer's description, is not a tree; it is something called a *semi-lattice*, a structure that permits overlapping sets. A route map of the United States is a semi-lattice; for example, New York is a member of the set of roads that connect New York . . . Chicago . . . Salt Lake City . . . Los Angeles *and at the same time* is a member of the set

* *The Macmillan Handbook of English*, Fifth Edition, by John M. Kierzek and Walker Gibson (New York: Macmillan, 1965).

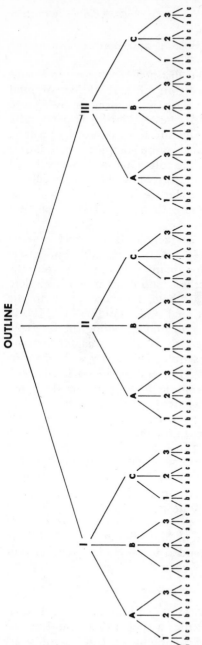

Figure 15. Textbook prose form structured as a "tree."

73

connecting New York, Boston, and Bangor, *and at the same time,* etc.

The importance of the distinction between trees and semi-lattices for the creation of a PMI/MS Manual resides not merely in overlap vs. non-overlap. Still more important is the fact that the semi-lattice is potentially a much more complex and subtle structure than a tree. We may see just how much more complex a semi-lattice can be than a tree is in the following fact: A tree based on 20 elements can contain at most 19 further subsets of the 20, whereas a semi-lattice based on the same 20 elements can contain more than one million different subsets.

The true problem thus emerges: It is to pick out the most functional linkages in the PMI/MS semi-lattice and to present them in a manner that will permit the reader to draw from these sub-structures a complete image of PMI/MS as a whole, in effect saying to the reader: Gaining a functional understanding of PMI/MS is something like coming to understanding the interconnections of a network of roads. If we imagine that no maps are available, we acquire familiarity with new surroundings simply by driving around in no fixed order from town to town (from node to node in the semi-lattice), making use of whatever road signs are available, and inevitably making a few redundant moves, until we are satisfied that we know how the land lies. A PMI/MS system must be explored in exactly the same way, and it was decided from the outset that no attempt should be made to structure the PMI/MS Manual according to the canons of the conventional expository medium, but rather to let the system lie as a network of towns and villages and to provide as comprehensive a set of road signs as the explorer might find himself in need of. The Manual is thus not intended to be read sequentially; it is to be *traversed.*

How do you find your way around a semi-lattice?

PMI/MS reveals itself through traversement.

Note 3

PMI/MS was created as a general purpose instructional control system, in particular a system that would not be dependent upon specific content, specific learning activities, or specific behavioral objectives. Its primary principle of design was that arbitrary skills learning materials, whether those of a commercial publishing house or those created specifically by a school, should be adaptable for use under a classroom peer-mediation system. Be this as it may, the Manual itself had to fulfill a teaching function, which is to say, in the words of the Introduction, it had to serve as a guide through a network of simulated experiences in the hope that in the process the learner would evolve a plan for creating totally new PMI/MS systems.

PMI/MS is not a set of instructional materials or texts: it is not competitive with textbooks or instructional media; it is a *management system for using existing instructional materials and texts.* PMI/MS bears the same relation to particular materials of instruction that a computer operating system bears to particular programing languages (e.g., FORTRAN) and content. A curriculum designer *programs* materials of instruction for use under PMI/MS. (As with a computer program, excellence of design is an ideal attained with a widely varying degree of success.)—PMI/MS Manual, 2.1.1.

Relation of a general purpose system to existing texts.

Still, the potential PMI/MS systems engineer must learn his trade by working through well-worked-out examples. No better example existed at the time when this work was started than the objectives and learning materials (and their implicit objectives) involved in the field test of PMI/MS that was to be carried out under the auspices of an operating company of the Bell System.

The first operational test of PMI/MS, upon which this manual is based, involved the use of the widely used language skills materials developed by MIND, Inc.* This large textbook, along with its associated tapes, was the basis of "English" instruction in the New York Telephone Company test environment. However, though the following descriptive discussion will be couched in terms of these MIND materials, *all* commercially available instructional materials for remedial reading and remedial basic language skills, as far as we are aware, can be adapted for PMI/MS use at marginal cost in time and effort.—PMI/MS Manual, 2.1.1.

* *MIND: Language Skills Development* (Stamford, Conn.: MIND, Inc., 1967).

What the Manual does is to characterize PMI/MS not in abstract terms, but in terms of a specific PMI/MS implementation.

There can be no question that if a more ideal Manual were to be created, it would contain numerous models of implementation. The Manual provided in this book is offered less as the last word in PMI/MS system design than as a comprehensive explication of a mature yet still evolving instructional system.

Note 4

In the sense that PMI/MS is a semi-lattice, an interesting circumstance arises in the fact that the Manual had to be *a manual*. For in a manual, every detail, if it is important at all, is *totally* important and must be given the same weight as every other such detail. Even so, decisions had to be made that would provide specific paths for the user to follow through the semi-lattice. From some vantage points it is possible to obtain a more immediately clear view than from others, as much as a high road view is apt to provide more information sooner than a low road view. Thus, in the creation of the Manual we selected what we considered to be a set of vantage points from which to survey the system and to provide cross-references to connect these various vantage points.

The view from the best vantage points.

Perspective 1. The first vantage point was that of the *classroom teacher,* in particular how this teacher would see the students in this class if they were spending their time under a PMI/MS system. Thus, the Manual explains that under PMI/MS a student performs either as a Teacher or as a Student and that at all times he is either one or the other. The Manual then explains specifically what students functioning as Students do; e.g., that they engage in either *independent activities* or *supervised activities.* Inasmuch as the exact nature of such activities depends upon the material being programed for PMI/MS use, the Manual illustrates the potential that is tapped by the MIND learning materials that were being used by the New York Telephone Company. First to be detailed are the independent activities, and they are discussed in terms of how the stu-

The classroom teacher's point of view.

dent's activities would appear to the classroom teacher if that student were working independently. Next to be described are the improvised activities in which a Student is seen to be working with his peer Teacher according to a structured dialogue.

Perspective 2. From another vantage point, the reader sees the facts of life under PMI/MS as they would be seen by the pupil functioning as Student. In particular, the reader understands that each Student is provided with a document that is both a road map and a checklist. As a road map, this document tells the Student what materials he is to use, how, and when. As a checklist, the document tells the Student where he has been and how far he has to go.

The Student's point of view.

Perspective 3. Here the reader learns how the sequence of PMI activities was created in the first place; in particular, how the implementor of PMI/MS goes about relating the syllabus of arbitrary instructional materials to PMI/MS sequence, which could be a process much the same as that for the MIND texts or one much richer.

Syllabus structure.

Perspective 4. This is the point of view of the pupil when he is functioning as a Teacher, what he is to do, how he is to do it, and the order in which he is to do things. Special attention is given to the details of the process by which the Teacher scores the performance of his Student.

The Teacher's point of view.

These four vantage points constitute what the Manual calls Details of Implementation. Another segment of the Manual surveys PMI/MS from the point of view of that hypothetical person in whom total responsibility for the administration and coordination of the system is invested, the person who must look after such matters as:

facilities
testing
starting up the system
scheduling
monitoring.

This section is called the Details of Administration. (This section contains one noteworthy structural error.

Three of the aspects of administration listed pertain not to administration of the system as a whole, but to the administration of particular classrooms by instructors. These relate to the procedure for pairing students, to the activities of the teacher when his student is engaged in independent learning activities, and to the global activities and options of the classroom instructor. These three should have formed their own subsection.)

The Manual also contains a short reference section that reviews *materials and personnel functions*. This section was not created so that it might be read in sequence. Rather, it is centrally located and fully cross-referenced so that the reader who finds himself in doubt on a particular physical or functional element of the system might find not only the definition of that element but also the full set of connections that bind it as an element in the system as a whole.

The curriculum planner's point of view.

Perhaps the most important point of view that is depicted is the point of view of the school staff member who would undertake to design and implement a PMI/MS system. This section informs the designer on what materials he needs; it tells him what to do to get started; it tells him how to update his system; and most important it provides a detailed model of an operating PMI/MS system in the form of a series of appendices that fully characterize the fixed components of the system when it was implemented by the New York Telephone Company. The Manual states:

> The quality of PMI/MS implementations is related, not surprisingly, to the experience of the designer. The best *initial* experience would be for the designer to use the body of this manual as a textbook, and to use the appendix material as a problem to be worked out. Appendices C and D are Student and Teacher Manuals based upon the content of the text material in Appendix A. Appendix E contains the correct answers for these materials. The PMI/MS syllabus designer should work with the text and appendices together until he is absolutely certain that he understands how the New York Telephone syllabus designers designed Appendices C and D on the basis of Appendix A.

Anyone who, having studied this manual, can understand

how Appendix C and Appendix D relate to Appendix A is capable in principle of designing and implementing a version of PMI/MS.

The central fact to keep in mind is that this manual is partially tailored for the MIND materials. Thus it is not the specific details of this particular MIND-based system that are crucial, but the basic elements of PMI/MS systems in general as they emerge from this implementation.—PMI/MS Manual, 5.1.

Notes on the Experimental Training Environment

Shortly after AT&T and Teachers College agreed to cooperate on the development and testing of the peer-mediation concept of instruction control, the New York Telephone Company was approached and offered the opportunity to participate in the project by providing an experimental environment. New York Telephone was ideal in two respects. The first was the relative proximity of the training environment to the head-quarters of the Teachers College research group (both in Manhattan). The second was the fact that this particular training environment housed one of the largest telephone company efforts in the remedial training area and was located in New York City, a location where, for the phone company, there existed a severe shortage of qualified manpower. If PMI was to prove its potential merit anywhere, where better than in New York City?

The AT&T Project (henceforth, the Project) had four operational stages. The first would see the design of a prototype of the Peer-Mediated Instruction/Management System. The second phase called upon the resources of Teachers College to perform an actual adaptation of specific materials of instruction for use under this system. System-wide, the Bell Companies employed five or six different brands of instructional materials for training in remedial language skills. The selection of texts was a completely discretionary matter, each company school exercising curricular autonomy. In the New York Telephone school, the language skills materials produced by MIND, Inc., were employed at the time as the basic English text. The MIND Language Skills textbook was organized

The AT&T Project phases.

around a sequence of "Skill Groups," one of which is replicated in Appendix A of the Manual. The MIND textbook was 438 pages long. MIND recommends that a course of 100 hours duration be organized around this textbook, and, indeed, the English course that was run at New York Telephone was assigned 100 contact hours. The task of this second phase was to adapt the MIND textbook for use under PMI/MS, performing the same task that a curriculum planner, consulting a manual, would be performing when adapting other materials of instruction for PMI/MS use.

The third phase was to try out the adaptation of the PMI/MS design for the MIND materials. The first tests were to be conducted at the Community Resources Center in East Harlem, operated by Teachers College's Horace Mann-Lincoln Institute. The students were volunteers from Brandeis High School and from Benjamin Franklin High School. The purpose of this phase was first to confirm whether the system would work at all and second to permit the debugging of the program as fully as possible before the full-scale test at New York Telephone.

And lastly would come the experiment itself at New York Telephone, where the phone company's instructional staff and the research staff from Teachers College would collaborate to change specific classroom procedure so as to permit the use of Peer-Mediated Instruction and where an entire class would be cycled through the program under this methodology.

A few words need to be said about the New York Telephone enviroment.

The experiment was carried out by the New York Telephone Company. The instructional environment employed for the trial was located in three classroom-sized rooms in a building in Manhattan owned by the New York Telephone Company. The students in the school were newly-hired employees of the Building and Supplies Division. They would go to jobs in building services, regardless of their academic progress in the school.

These employees were hired by the phone company on an exceptional basis; their performance on the qualifying tests that are administered to all prospective employees

of the Bell System was below standard cutoffs. When
tested on reading tests such as the Stanford Achievement Details.
Test (Intermediate Level) and the Nelson Test, scores
placing in a range from third grade to ninth grade reading level were being achieved by the employees, with the
average around sixth grade.

It was the purpose of this innovative program to ele-
vate the educational attainment of these special employees as measured by the Bell System Qualifying Test
(BSQT), a test considered by the Bell System to be related to an employee's ability to absorb knowledge and
to perform his job successfully. School was in session from
8:00 a.m. until 5:00 p.m., Monday through Friday. The
course of instruction lasted for eight weeks, during which
time 100 instructional hours were reserved for instruction in English and 100 for instruction in Math. The
school served another purpose of equal importance, The NYT
which was to strengthen the overall effort to encourage school's
new employees to pursue long-term careers in the phone purposes.
company. In this regard, the school served as a buffer
in which points of conflict between the "real" world and
the "world of work" could be resolved or at least cush-
ioned before new employees arrived on the job out in
the field. Such buffering was accomplished in two ways. Technique.
First, two hours a day of instruction were specifically devoted to a subject matter, called "World of Work," in
which were presented a variety of subjects (e.g., budget-
ing, medical care, drugs, getting along with supervisor),
through a variety of different mediational processes (e.g.,
encounter, role play, lecture, rap session), using various
pieces of audio-visual hardware (e.g., tape recorders,
video tape). Second, the school itself was a job environment. The classroom instructors were line managers
and had the relation of supervisor-supervisee to the students in the school. Thus, as a job environment the
school was real; but in an academic sense, it was not "for
real," since no one could flunk out for unsatisfactory
academic performance. The students were employees paid
to go to school.

The teachers in the school, called "trainers," were
selected for their training positions because of their

The trainers were good, intelligent, resourceful people. leadership qualities and their promised personal effectiveness in relating to the emotional and educational needs of the student population. This philosophy of teacher selection indeed appeared to have had the consequence of bringing about a high level of rapport and productive understanding between trainer and trainee.

4

The Experiment

Creating the Population Samples

The crucial purpose of the experiment conducted at
New York Telephone was to establish the efficacy of the
PMI concept relative to the remedial instructional practices then being followed, practices considered to be
representative of those in use throughout the Bell System. Fulfilling such purpose calls for an experimental
form that includes, as one of its procedures, the establishment of two subject populations, "samples," that are
comparable in all respects thought to be relevant. Each
group is exposed to one of the two methodologies being
compared; and differences between the groups resulting
from the treatments are then sought. The way in which
the samples are initially created may vary considerably
according to the circumstances of the experiment. Sometimes, for example, it is possible actually to create two
samples from a single on-hand pool of subjects, on
analogy to what a teacher does in choosing up teams
for a classroom competition. This is a most desirable
kind of procedure because it allows the researcher to
exercise quite rigid control over the distribution of
critical variables, e.g., age, sex, aptitude, background,
etc., in the two groups. The researcher can ensure, in
advance, that he will have comparable experimental
("subject") and reference ("control") populations. Un-

What would
have been
nice!

fortunately, this approach to sample selection was not feasible in the New York Telephone environment.

The issue faced at New York Telephone stemmed from the reluctance of the school's R & D staff to subdivide a class into those who would take the PMI version of the course and those who would take the conventional version. It was believed (and correctly so to view the project in retrospect) that if the class was broken into two groups, on any basis whatever, the students would feel that they were secretly being experimented with. The expressed policy of the school, i.e., openness, honesty, and sincerity in all dealings with students, would possibly be threatened by a student awareness of being treated as guinea pigs. Quite aside from the politics of the situation, it must also be mentioned that a subdivision of a single class into PMI/MS group and Control group would have a certain statistical disadvantage in that the size of each group could be no more than 17 or 18 (assuming 10% attrition during the term of instruction). Thus, the hope of creating samples from the single student population that would be in residence during one cycle of eight weeks had to be abandoned. In its place came the idea of using a class having previously finished as the Control sample, in particular the December class, that had been graduated from the school two weeks prior to the start-up date for the experimental class (February 1971).

In terms of test-measured ability, the December 1970 class and the February 1971 class were very similar. To determine whether any evidence existed to the effect that the two groups were *not* initially comparable on those criterion measures* that New York Telephone had selected as indicators of reading ability, pre-treatment mean scores were compared by *t* tests for two independent samples. The results of these analyses, given in Table 2, show that no significant differences existed be-

But, the experimental class could not be subdivided.

---

* Stanford Achievement Test (Intermediate Level) Vocabulary and Comprehension; Nelson Test Vocabulary and Comprehension. The process through which these measures were selected is discussed in the following section.

Table 2. Comparison of pre-treatment mean raw scores on four
factors of reading ability: PMI/MS and Control groups.

Factors	PMI/MS		Control		t value
	Mean	SD	Mean	SD	
	(N=35)		(N=23)		
1. SAT Vocabulary	25.3	8.7	22.1	7.0	−1.67 (NS)
2. SAT Comprehension	31.8	9.1	28.3	8.7	−1.62 (NS)
	(N=35)		(N=30)		
3. Nelson Vocabulary	40.7	12.9	38.1	15.5	−0.74 (NS)
4. Nelson Comprehension	28.1	9.6	26.7	12.6	−0.51 (NS)

NS—Not significant at .05 level.

tween the groups, substantiating the claim that an
equivalence existed between the groups that could have
existed had the two groups been selected randomly from
a common pool.

On all four factors of reading ability there is a tendency
for the PMI/MS group's scores to exceed the control
group's, although these differences have no statistical
significance. In other words, the observed differences
represent a statistical accident resulting from testing
error. It is still possible, however, that such differences
really do represent an initial inequality between the
groups at the outset of their instructional experiences.
And for this reason, a higher consideration should be
voiced. Translated into grade equivalents, as both SAT
and Nelson tests allow, the mean differences on all four
variables are all less than one-half a grade level. The
plain fact is that, relative to the kind of mean differences
or efficiency increases that a curriculum policy maker
would have to be shown if he were going to recommend
the permanent use of PMI/MS, a one-fourth grade level
difference overall would no doubt be seen, and in fact
was seen by phone company personnel, to be negligibly
small. This, coupled with the great ethnic similarity
between the two groups, led us to accept that in all important respects these groups were sufficiently similar
that one might reasonably attribute any post-treatment
differences to the treatment itself rather than to pre-existing differences between the subject populations.

Similarity of experimental and control groups.

Selecting Criteria for Judging Outcomes

The AT&T sponsors of the New York Telephone project were willing to accept that qualitative as well as quantita‑ tive comparisons should be made, particularly to the extent that they involved student and faculty attitudes toward classroom experiences under a PMI system. It is doubtful, however, whether any qualitative outcome, no matter how favorable, could alone have induced a switchover to PMI in the face of negative, neutral, or even low-level positive quantitative differences. The test of quantitative improvement was felt by phone company personnel to be crucial, both in New York Telephone and in AT&T. Thus a great deal of attention had to be given to the issue of what kinds of measurements would be made.

Issues of measurement involve a high level of linguis‑ tic precision. Discussions were conducted with the NYT R&D staffs to find out what the goal skills of "English" actually were, what "English" was all about. As it turned out, the focus of "English" was "Reading," defined by New York Telephone as consisting at least in part of

Necessity of
using tests
then in use. two quantitative components. The first of these was "Vocabulary," as measured by both of the two standard‑ ized tests then in use at New York Telephone: the Nelson Test and the Intermediate Level of the Stanford Achieve‑ ment Test. The second component was "Comprehen‑ sion," as measured also by these same test instruments. (These tests have similarities and dissimilarities, but procedurally they have much in common. Each contains a short timed sub-test of the subject's knowledge of the meaning of words. And each contains a short, timed sub-test of the subject's ability to answer questions based on a prose passage.) It had been the practice at New York Telephone to administer both of these tests, the Nelson and the SAT, to all students prior to any instruc‑ tional experience and, subsequently upon the student's completion of the instructional sequence, to administer a different form of the same test. And the difference scores ($posttest - pretest = difference\ score$) between the pretest and the posttest scores were used by the R&D

staff in evaluating and accounting for performance improvements. These same indicators were to be used during the experimental use of the PMI system.

As noted earlier, it *had* to be that the entire subject class would be a PMI class, and a class having already finished the course and graduated from the school would serve as the control population. This meant that no tests that had not been used for the earlier class could possibly be used for the experimental class. Although a few *criterion reference* tests had been administered to the December 1971 class, records had been retained only for the major standardized tests.

Unavoidable testing inflexibility.

A further refinement was suggested by consideration of a distinction that exists between a *test* proper and a *syllabus* proper. The descriptive power of any test obviously depends upon the extent to which the content *and* the mediating activities of the test representatively sample the course content, as embodied in the materials of instruction, and its mediating procedures, as embodied in learning activities. The greater the degree of mismatch along either of these two dimensions, content or mediation, between the test and the course proper, the less is that test a test of what has been taught. Now, this fact has certain obvious consequences, for if in some particular instance there does indeed exist a gap between what a test tests and what the environment teaches, then no positive results can either be anticipated or expected. No amount of spelling instruction will produce positive results on a calculus test. The rub is this: This dilemma seems almost to be perpetual and PMI/MS *does nothing* to alter the situation, for it does not alter the content or basic activity format of the instructional materials to which it is applied. Thus, if the Nelson Test and the SAT do not test what a certain course of instruction in reality teaches, there is absolutely no reason to expect that the mere use of PMI is going to lead to measurably improved learning (faster, perhaps, but not improved). The system may in fact be producing substantial learning increases in what the course teaches. But since there exists no test that tests what the course teaches, this fact cannot be known. So, any comparative test used to evaluate the effectiveness of the PMI methodology must come reasonably close to being a test of actual course content.

Through an examination of the course materials then being tried out by New York Telephone, i.e., the MIND textbook and its associated tapes, an unacceptably large gap became apparent between the comprehension components of the two achievement tests, on the one hand, and the curriculum of the MIND text, on the other. The comprehension task in these standardized tests involves reading a short prose passage and selecting the correct answers to several objective questions about the passage from a given set. There is nothing unusual about the mediating process that engages the student on these two tests; it is actually a stereotype, finding virtually universal use whenever "comprehension" is tested. The MIND textbook did not contain comparable sequences of learning activities, however. Assuming that students learn to do what they do as they learn, consider that at no point in the MIND course did students actually practice reading comprehension as this skill is implicitly defined by the mediating processes of the test. Thus there could really be no reason to expect that the course, as it was or could be given, even under PMI/MS, would lead to measured improvement in comprehension. And so it appeared to make no sense to rely upon, or even use, the Comprehension sub-tests in the evaluation of PMI as applied to MIND.

Lack of match-up between materials and tests for Comprehension.

Our decision not to use the Comprehension sub-tests was not based entirely on an assumedly imperfect match between the test and the syllabus; also involved was the substantiating fact that the Control class, along with any other earlier class, had shown relatively little growth in Comprehension ability, as measured by these sub-tests, certainly much less growth than a curriculum planner might reasonably hope to achieve as the result of the 100 hours of instruction. As Figure 16 shows, however, quantitatively very little learning had indeed occurred for the Control class along the Comprehension dimension; moreover, and perhaps more importantly, Control group performance in Comprehension was notably inferior to their performance in Vocabulary.

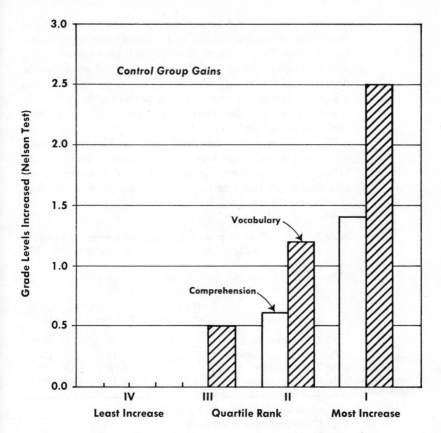

Figure 16. Number of grade levels gained by Control group in Comprehension and Vocabulary. Zero improvement is to be noted for the IVth and IIIrd quartiles in Comprehension. Zero improvement is also noted for the IVth quartile in Vocabulary.

The chart blocks Control group students into quartiles based upon the number of grade levels (derived from published test norms) increased, that is, students' pretest grade level scores subtracted from their posttest grade level scores. Two sets of scores are plotted, those for the Comprehension sub-test and those for the Vocabulary sub-test of the Nelson Test.

Notice, first, that for the bottom of the Control class, there was no improvement in Comprehension whatever. In the top 25%, where gains could be expected, the average improvement was no better than 1.4 grade levels. For the class over all, the average was no better than 0.5 grade levels, an amount that probably exceeds only slightly, if at all, the testing error on the Nelson Comprehension sub-test.

Not only was the learning gain in Comprehension small by practical standards, it was possible furthermore to argue that whatever gains had been observed along this dimension had been a statistical accident, as the fact of non-significant t values in Table 3 suggests.

Table 3. Comparison of pretest and posttest means on four factors of reading ability: Control group only (N=33).

Factors	Mean Difference (Pretest-Posttest)	St. Dev	t value
1. SAT Comprehension	1.27	10.50	0.696 (NS)
2. Nelson Comprehension	1.03	7.31	0.774 (NS)
3. SAT Vocabulary	5.06	8.18	3.55 **
4. Nelson Vocabulary	6.27	8.32	4.125 ***

Indeed, results in comprehension had never been observed.

NS—Not significant at .05 level.
**—Significant at .01 level.
***—Significant at .001 level.

We therefore decided not to make use of the Comprehension sub-test as an evaluative instrument in the study, for in the event that positive comprehension data were not generated, we would have no way of knowing whether to attribute this outcome to PMI/MS or to MIND.

This left us with but one criterion for evaluative testing, the Vocabulary sub-tests on the Nelson and the SAT. Here we were fortunate. For one thing, the MIND materials, even though oriented toward so-called "word attack" activities, provided a very extensive vocabulary component, introducing several thousand words distributed throughout the units of the text. For another, many of the MIND learning activities did, in fact, call for the use of these words; hence, students had to be involved with these words to a relatively great extent. It could thus reasonably be argued that MIND tried to teach vocabulary in substantially the same manner that the tests test it. Indeed, the grade level achievement of the Control class students in vocabulary greatly exceeded the performance of that same class in comprehension, as is recorded in Table 3. Furthermore, one can observe in Figure 16 that the performance differences in Vocabulary are strikingly greater than and contrast tellingly with the performance of the same group in Comprehension.

On the basis of these considerations, we decided to make do with the vocabulary sub-tests as criterion measures to evaluate PMI/MS performance relative to Control performance. It appeared that MIND did indeed strive to teach a vocabulary content, success in the acquisition of which could be measured by standardized tests. And so, if PMI/MS did represent a superior methodology for addressing that content, this superiority ought to be reflected in superior grade level increases for the students using this methodology over those who did not.

We make do with vocabulary.

Since the value of instructional gains derived from the use of a new methodology is necessarily relative to the degree of effort needed to achieve these gains, it is reasonable to measure not just the performance variables themselves, but also the components of effort related to these variables. In many such respects, the PMI/MS and the control methodologies were comparable, i.e., for both, the cost of materials was comparable, PMI/MS being exclusively a software technology; for both, the presence of a classroom instructor was required, albeit that the roles played by this instructor were quite different in the two cases; for both, the costs of facilities and administrative overhead were comparable. But in one crucial respect, the competing programs could well be expected to be quite different; and this respect is one of *time*.

The measurement of effort.

Learning time measured as well as performance. Under the Control methodology, student participation in English was required for 100 hours, regardless of whether particular students could have completed the syllabus sooner. The Control class was paced *as a class;* the classroom instructor would establish and maintain a uniform rate of progress through the MIND syllabus. PMI/MS, however, transfers both the prerogatives and responsibilities of pacing student progress from the classroom instructor to the students themselves. The student goes as fast as his performance allows. And so, it seemed not only possible, but indeed likely, that some, if not most, of the students of the PMI/MS class would complete the syllabus in less than the 100 hours that had been imposed upon their Control group counterparts. The trainers themselves felt that this might be the case since, by their own account, they tended to accomodate the pacing of the class to the apparent pace of the weaker students. And so, it was agreed that we would keep a careful record of how long it took individual students to complete the program in terms of *hours of PMI/MS instruction.* With such information available, it would become possible to examine PMI/MS not just with regard to gross instructional output but also with regard to relative economy of effort.

Procedures

Schedule

The plan of the experiment called for the PMI/MS class to follow the schedule of the Control class identically. This would mean that during the course of the eight-week session, 100 instructional hours would be allotted for English; furthermore, that each week would see 12 to 15 hours of instruction with 2 to 3 hours on any given day. When during the day and in what quantities English was to be given were posted on a schedule one week in advance. Every three-hour session would be punctuated by a fifteen-minute coffee break.

Students were not to be introduced to PMI/MS until the second week of instruction, the first week being largely devoted to testing, counseling, and orientation activities. Toward the latter part of the first week, stu-

dents were introduced to the MIND textbook that they
would be using, but not until Monday of the second
week did orientation to PMI/MS actually begin. We
planned that PMI/MS operation would be fully under
way by Wednesday of that second week, assuming that 4
to 6 hours of prior PMI/MS orientation would be sufficient to permit smooth functioning of the system.

Observations

It was agreed between the Teachers College research
group and the New York Telephone curricular staff that
PMI/MS operations would be monitored in three ways.
The first was simply direct classroom observation by the
classroom instructors, who would, on a continuous
basis, keep the TC staff informed on the details of
classroom activity, what was going well, what needed
improvement, where potential problems might reside, etc.
The second was daily recording of student progress via **Three modes**
the Scoring Forms turned in (see p. 253) during the **of monitoring.**
course of a PMI/MS session. These records would make
it possible to study the rates of student progress in terms
of MIND units completed per unit of time. And thus,
we would be able to project completion dates and
determine the accuracy and reliability of these projec-
tions. Third was the installation of so-called "criterion"
tests into the PMI/MS-MIND syllabus; these were
selective achievement tests on MIND materials covered
in a recent unit. These tests were intended to be used
as real-time indicators of the current viability of the
PMI/MS method. If anything was going haywire from an
instructional point of view, these tests would surely show
it.

Outside observers of classes were not encouraged. This
policy was not adopted, however, just for the purpose of
the experiment, for it had been a tenet of the school's
philosophy from its founding days that students should
not be made to feel they were in a fishbowl. Thus,
with the exception of one visit from the AT&T sponsors and one visit from a photographer, the PMI/MS
students encountered no strangers in the instructional
environment.

What Students Were Told

The entering class of 39 students was subdivided by the school staff into 3 classes of 13 on the basis of the *overall* SAT grade level average (including Math as well as English skills). The students were given no information about the use of PMI/MS that would in any way suggest that the instructional experience the students were about to undergo was out of the ordinary, or in any way different from the experience of previous classes. The two TC staff members who were to be on-site virtually full time were identified during the first day's orientation meeting as assistants to the trainers.

Nothing out of the ordinary.

Classroom Teachers

First, a general remark about classroom teachers ("trainers") at the New York Telephone school. It should be kept in mind that academic achievement was only one dimension of the mission that the remedial training group at New York Telephone was pursuing. A basic goal was to stimulate a cultural adjustment for students, from the culture generally of a ghetto to the culture of the phone company. In this mission, the performance of the instructional staff of the school had been outstanding. At various times in the recent past, the retention rate of graduates from the school in the company (often with advancement) after one year has exceeded 80%, a figure that was believed to significantly exceed the performance of other industrial training programs. I am quite convinced that this remarkable performance can be directly attributed to the affective characteristics of the trainers, their impressive ability to relate meaningfully to the trainees. Indeed, not one of the five trainers who ultimately participated in the project had had professional preparation or experience in teaching; all had been supervisory employees in the operating division of New York Telephone. (This is a useful point to bear in mind in assessing the outcome of the project, for it bears directly on the matter of the facility with which PMI systems can be administered.)

Trainers had been selected previously for their affective traits.

Two weeks prior to the start of the PMI/MS cycle, the TC staff conducted a 1½ day orientation on PMI/MS teaching for the three trainers who were going to teach the three sections. This orientation was conducted in the following way:

First, the trainers were given a copy of the PMI/MS manual to read (in fact, the fore-runner of the one at the end of this book) in the presence of the TC staff, who were there to answer questions as they might come up in the course of the reading. Second, the trainers acted out Teacher and Student roles. Third, the trainers were asked to reflect overnight on the PMI/MS operating procedure and to come prepared the next morning for a complete review, at which all remaining questions would be answered.

Orientation was minimal.

For the orientation of trainees as well as the classroom administration of PMI/MS, the trainers were given total discretionary power. The TC staff that was on hand served basically a consulting role.

Of the three teachers assigned to the three sections, two had taught classes previously, the third had not. Two additional teachers, who were to be assigned to their own classes during the cycle subsequent to the PMI/MS cycle, arrived during the course of the PMI/MS cycle. With the prospect that PMI/MS might become justifiable as a permanent instructional methodology, the director of the school assigned these two new teachers to learn PMI/MS operating procedures via a sitting-in method. Within a few days, these new teachers were well enough versed in technique that they could and often did substitute for the original teachers. These substitutions were carried out apparently without any noticeably unfortunate instructional effects, a fact of some interest in view of the particular difficulties associated with teacher substitution in public schools.

Tests

As noted previously, two batteries of tests were to be employed. The Nelson Test (Form A) was administered at the school during the first week, the orientation phase,

Table 4. Mean pre-post change on two factors of reading ability: Control group.

Factors	Mean Change	St. Dev.	*t* value
1. SAT Vocabulary	5.06	8.18	3.55**
2. Nelson Vocabulary	6.27	8.32	4.125***

**—Significant at .01 level.
***—Significant at .001 level.

by staff members of the school. Form B was administered at the school during the final week by representatives of the New York Telephone personnel office, summoned specially for their presumed impartiality. The Stanford Achievement Test (Form X) was administered at a New York Telephone personnel office prior to assignment to the school. Form Y was administered at the school by personnel office representatives during the final week, on the day following the Nelson Test (Form B).

The Findings

Before asking the most interesting question, whether there had occurred significantly greater learning for the PMI/MS group than for the Control group, it is of some interest to inquire whether statistically significant growth occurred for the two groups considered separately. These questions can be answered by analyzing the mean change scores, the result of subtracting pre- from posttest mean scores, via *t* tests for dependent samples. The results are shown in Tables 4 and 5.

It is clear that both groups of students achieved statistically significant increases in Vocabulary skill as

Table 5. Mean pre-post change on two factors of reading ability: PMI/MS group.

Factors	Mean Change	St. Dev.	*t* value
1. SAT Vocabulary	9.66	5.67	10.07***
2. Nelson Vocabulary	12.49	9.30	7.94***

***—Significant at .001 level.

measured by the Stanford Achievement Test and the Nelson Test. Thus, the primary hypothesis becomes all the more interesting: that the PMI/MS group will perform significantly higher on the Vocabulary factor in reading ability than will the Control group. Again a *t* test comparison was employed, this time involving the posttest mean scores for the two groups. Table 6 shows the results of these comparisons.

Both groups improved as the result of treatment.

Table 6. Comparison of posttest mean scores on two factors of reading ability: Control and PMI/MS.

Factors	Control		PMI/MS		*t* value	df
	Mean	SD	Mean	SD		
1. SAT Vocabulary	27.15	10.00	34.97	9.70	3.266**	66
2. Nelson Vocabulary	44.33	16.28	53.14	11.54	2.542*	63

**Significant at .01 level.
*Significant at .02 level.

PMI/MS superior to Control.

It is evident from the *t* values in Table 4 that the PMI/MS group had established a quite significant superiority over the Control group in its performance on the Vocabulary sub-tests of both the Stanford Achievement Test and the Nelson Test. But the most important fact to emerge from the findings of the New York Telephone study was not that the PMI/MS methodology should prove statistically superior—this was expected. More important, in a sense that becomes paramount in the making of curricular decisions, the magnitude of PMI/MS's superiority was very great indeed.

But the real question is, "how big" are the differences?

The Magnitude of the Difference

The central measure by which an instructional method should be tested is not, foremost, the level of achievement that results from the use of the method, but rather the *extent* of achievement, that is, how far the student has come as the direct result of his instructional experience. In other words, we are less interested here in whether these end points were significantly different for Control and PMI/MS classes than we are in how much advancement in ability has occurred for the two groups.

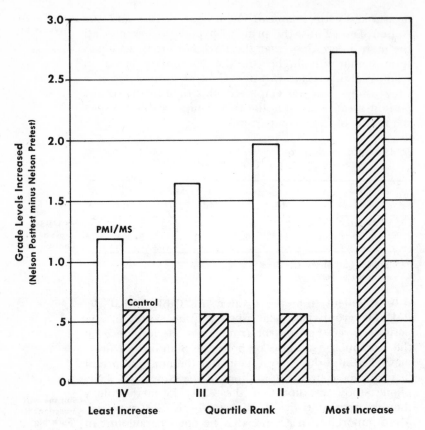

Figure 17. Gross instructional gain in vocabulary.

The units of achievements in the New York Telephone project could be stated either in terms of the raw scores presented by the criterion tests, the SAT and Nelson Test, or in terms of the grade level norms into which the raw scores can be translated. We use the latter in the following discussion since grade level norms were the indices used by the New York Telephone staff.

Let us review the outcome of the experiment in terms of the extent of improvement as measured by the Nelson

Test. Figure 17 was constructed in the following manner: for each student in each group, Control and PMI/MS, that student's pretest grade level score was subtracted from his posttest score. For each group of students, these "difference" scores were then placed in rank order and blocked into quartiles. For each quartile, an average difference score was computed and plotted.

First the reader's attention is directed to the distribution of the Control group. In particular notice how high the average increase score for the first quartile is relative to the average score for the lower three quartiles —2.4 grade levels as compared with 0.6 grade levels for each of the three lower quartiles. Notwithstanding the statistical significance of the performance improvement for the Control group taken as a whole, it would appear that a very substantial increase in learning has occurred for 25% of the Control class, but that very little has occurred for 75%. Certainly in the dollars and cents terms of the telephone company, a one-half grade level vocabulary improvement after 100 hours of instruction could not reasonably occasion any back-patting. Indeed, the performance of three-fourths of the Control class is uniformly undistinguished. Even the fact that the performance increase for the top one-fourth of the Control group is substantial most probably does not mean that the Control methodology was selectively effective. Rather, it would not be surprising that this distributional peculiarity has its basis in the common phenomenon of instructional research whereby a certain percentage of *every* class seems to do well regardless of treatment. There are always some students who seem to learn no matter what. Of course the same consideration would hold for the top one-fourth of the PMI/MS class. If it is true, however, that it is these students who go to make up the majority in the first quartile of the Control group, then we may say that, with the notable exception of this group, the Control methodology has proven to be relatively ineffective.

Control group performance is undistinguished.

It is immediately apparent from the chart that the PMI/MS group performed in a superior manner to the Control population *across the board*. Even in the segment of the class containing students with the least impressive performance improvement, the fourth quartile, the average grade level increase of the PMI/MS group doubled that of the Control group, 1.2 grade levels as compared with 0.6 grade levels. In the third quartile, the ratio is better than 2.5:1; and in the second quartile, better than 3:1. Only in the first quartile, which for both groups no doubt contains students who would achieve even under marginal instructional conditions, is the performance difference between PMI/MS and Control relatively unsubstantial (2.8 to 2.3 grade levels in favor of the PMI/MS group). If the top quartile is excluded from consideration, the average difference in grade level improvement between PMI/MS and Control slightly exceeds one entire grade level (1.63 to 0.6). Thus, statistical significance notwithstanding, the Control methodology has apparently had little pay-off for the majority of the Controls; certainly, the pay-off for the group undergoing the PMI/MS treatment has been considerably greater.

PMI/MS class improves "across-the-board."

But, even this is not by any means the entire story. The performance differences between PMI/MS and Control become even more impressive when viewed in light of the fact that the minimal gains of the Control population took 100 hours of instruction, no more, no less, to achieve, for the Controls experienced a lock-step methodology. It should come as no surprise, therefore, that scores reported in Table 5 for the PMI/MS group were generated in less, and frequently considerably less, than 100 hours (see Figure 18). And so, the performance differences reported in Figure 17 should be valued even more highly than our initial appraisal would suggest. Indeed, the relation of learning time to instructional output is worth investigating in greater detail.

Enter the factor of learning time.

Since we have an achievement score (grade levels increased) and a time-to-completion score for each student in the PMI/MS and Control classes, we can construct a ratio that says something about each student's learning power as demonstrated exclusively during the learning experience at New York Telephone, in particular about the number of hours of instruction that are entailed by

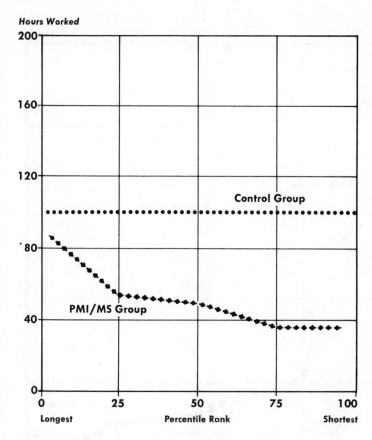

Figure 18. Learning times to completion.

the achievement of a *one* grade level improvement. Note well that this score does not in any way imply that John Doe actually did advance one measurable grade level in a specific block of time. Nor does it imply that John Doe could be expected to progress at that rate regardless of his position in the syllabus; a deceleration is certainly to be expected with exposure to increasingly complex material. Nor, finally, does it state that any two students with the same score are comparable either in

Hours Worked

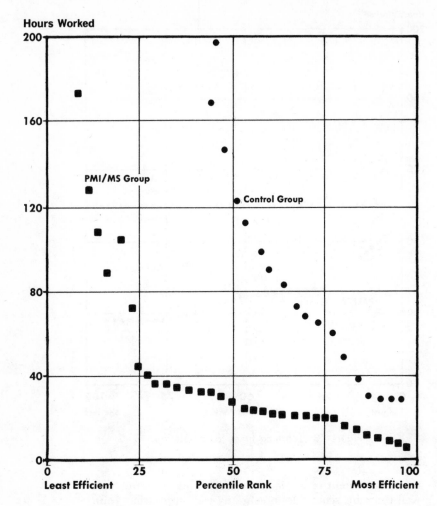

Figure 19. Hours worked per grade level achieved.

aptitude or in achievement. Still, given the number of
grade levels increased for each student and the number of
hours that it took each student to achieve that increase,
it becomes possible, subject to the exercise of reasonable
caution in interpretation, to contrast control and experimental methodologies in terms of learning *efficiency*, i.e.,
quantity of learning per unit time spent in learning
activities. Efficiency scores, i.e., hours worked divided by
grade levels advanced, can be generated for members of
the Control and PMI/MS classes. These scores have
utility, for they can establish for the management of the
school a comparison between competing methodologies
that expresses quantity of learning system output as a
function of how much time an employee might be away
from his regular assignment for instructional purposes;
how economically, in other words, two systems have performed on a standardized task to bring a student up one
measured grade level in a standardized test. When these
efficiency scores are ranked and plotted, they reveal an
interesting pattern.

Efficiency scores computed.

In Figure 19, the lower a plotted point is, the more
productively instructional time is being spent by the
student represented by that point. The *most* productive
student in the Control class advanced one grade level
for each 28 hours spent in instruction. Perhaps the single
most dramatic feature of the graph is this: The very best
efficiency score in the Control group is 28 hours per
grade level achieved. Indeed, three students in the
Control class achieved this score. But in the PMI/MS
class, *fully 50% of the entire class did better than the
best Control student.* No less dramatic: In the nominal
100 hours of instruction at New York Telephone, 85%
of the PMI/MS class advanced a grade level or more as
compared with 42% of the Control class.

Figure 20 shows the relative efficiency of the two
methodologies as a function of varying numbers of hours
of instruction.

These interpretations have been presented publicly
a number of times, in industrial and other educational
settings, and have generally been accepted as evidence
of the instructional power of peer-mediated instructional

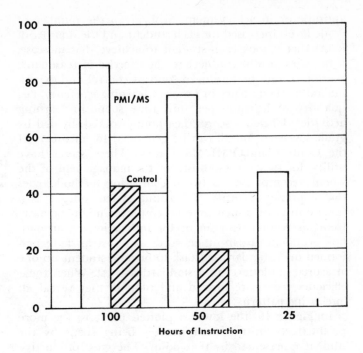

Figure 20. Efficiency: Percentage achieving one grade level increase vs. hours of instruction.

systems. Indeed, there seemed little question in the minds of the New York Telephone staff that the use of PMI/MS should be continued in succeeding instructional cycles. In fact, further applications of PMI were under active consideration for implementation, subject to budgetary limitation. These additional applications were to include the conversion of the mathematics component of the curriculum to a PMI/MS system and, to take advantage of the time savings created by PMI/MS-MIND, to upgrade the English program with a PMI/MS version of instructional materials specifically designed to instruct in the comprehensional aspect of reading, so that between MIND and these new materials, both vocabulary and comprehension would be adequately covered.

CHAPTER 5

An In-Service Application: The Jackson PMI Project

As this manuscript enters the final stages of editing, the initial phase of a PMI project is being completed in the public school system of Jackson, Mississippi. The reader will find a report of preliminary findings in a letter to Dr. Brandon Sparkman, Superintendent of Instruction for Jackson, that is appended to this chapter. The project is worth reviewing, for unlike either the P.S. 129 or New York Telephone projects, which were carried through under the intensive supervision of Teachers College personnel, the Jackson PMI system was designed, implemented, and managed exclusively by in-service staff of the Jackson School System, that is to say, by practitioners. Thus, the Jackson PMI project provides a model that can be tapped by school personnel as a practical guide to the development of PMI systems.

Background

Shortly after the termination of the New York Telephone project, I was asked by AT&T's Department of

Environmental Affairs, the agency that had supported the development of PMI/MS, to make a presentation on the project to the management staff of the South Central Bell Telephone Company in Jackson and also to the man who has since become the Superintendent of Instruction in Jackson, Dr. Brandon Sparkman. In holding this meeting, it was South Central Bell's intention to explore ways in which the Jackson Public Schools and South Central Bell might work together on the problems of education in relation to the world of work. This included a presentation on PMI as an approach to remedial education. Some weeks after this presentation, I received a call from Jackson asking whether I would be willing and able to manage a PMI project at the secondary level in the Jackson Public Schools with a target subject matter of remedial reading. I replied that I did not have the time available to undertake the *direct* supervision of such a project but that I thought the job could be done quite

PMI development as an in-service effort. effectively by an in-service staff whom I might instruct in the principles and mechanics of Peer-Mediated Instruction and whom I could supervise in the implementation and application of these. This proposal was accepted by the Jackson in-service staff as a suitable basis for a project and, consequently, a project was designed.

The project called for PMI to be employed in three schools, four classes in each school, each class with its own instructor. For each of the three schools, a PMI Facilitator (each a reading specialist) was appointed. The general responsibilities of the Facilitators were: (1) to work directly with me on the PMI system design; (2) to implement requisite software; (3) to supervise installation of the physical components of the system; and (4) to provide the PMI classroom instructors with orientational and administrative support. In other words, the PMI

PMI: Is it for real, or is it a laboratory curiosity? and administrative support. In other words, the PMI Facilitators would be the key figures in the project. If they could successfully implement a PMI system, then it would be satisfactorily established that PMI is a practical classroom technology; if they could not, then some considerable doubt would exist as to whether PMI could ever be more than a laboratory curiosity.

The Facilitators' Initial Exposure to PMI

The project began officially with a two-day workshop conducted by me for the three PMI Facilitators, the agenda for which was roughly as follows:

1. to establish minimal conditions of adequacy for effective pedagogy
2. to demonstrate how PMI meets these conditions
3. to discuss issues relating to implementation
4. to design a PMI system
5. to ascertain and assign the work to be done
6. to plan instructor orientation.

The planning workshop.

What follows is a synopsis of the presentation and discussion.

External Conditions of Adequacy

Instructional strategies fail for a wide variety of reasons, many of which are recognized or at least intuited by classroom teachers. Three causes of failure are typical of conventional skills instruction. Specifically, conventional systems of skills instruction *fix the pace* of instruction; they *do not insist on mastery;* and they *do not provide* students with *rapid and detailed feedback* to trainees on the adequacy of their performance or to instructors on the adequacy of their instruction.

The consequences of these shortcomings are succinctly outlined in the "instructional principles" presented by Weingarten in a HUMRRO (Human Resources Research Organization) Professional Paper,* from which I quote or paraphrase freely in the following few paragraphs.

For various reasons, including differential aptitude, some people are capable of learning faster than are

---

* "The Development of a Low-Cost Performance-Oriented Training Model," by Kenneth Weingarten, Jacklyn Hungerland, Mark Brennon, and Brent Allred, Professional Paper 32-70 (Alexandria, Va.: HUMRRO, December 1970).

others. Instructional methods that fix the pace at which learning must take place will generally leave some students behind and bore others. Although the need for self-pacing is somewhat less urgent for "homogeneous" groups (especially those comprising students high on the educational and aptitudinal scales), no group of people is ever perfectly homogeneous. Consequently, *self-pacing is desirable in any training effort.* The weaknesses of fixed-pace training methods are most clearly demonstrated by the frequency with which large numbers of students fail to master the skills they are being taught. Differential achievement in training is the inevitable result of attempts to force everyone to learn at the same rate. But fixed pace instruction is so commonly practiced that many have come to the conclusion that differential achievement is an inevitable consequence of all training. Experience has demonstrated, however, that when students can proceed at rates appropriate to their various capabilities, the great majority can attain high levels of achievement.

Need for self-pacing.

The feature of self-pacing may be necessary to any effective training effort, but it is not sufficient. A book is a self-pacing instructional device, but, as Thorndike noted, its use in the prescribed manner does not guarantee subject matter mastery. It is frequently alleged that programed instruction offers little improvement on the conventional textbook in this regard inasmuch as it relies on students to assess their own mastery of the subject. Students, it is felt, are somwhat predisposed to give themselves the benefit of the doubt on questions of mastery with the consequent result that less, often considerably less, is learned than might be hoped. If self-pacing is to be incorporated effectively into a training system, *provision must be made for determining whether a student's performance has reached a stipulated level of mastery before he is permitted to proceed to the next learning task.* This kind of rigorous quality control is the *sine qua non* of any efficient instructional model.

Need for insistence on mastery.

Training methods that permit only delayed feedback in the form of end-of-cycle exams, for example, tend to compound mislearning and will often produce negative effects on motivation. It is always preferable for students to experience a sense of security in what they have already learned before going on to learn something else. This implies that accurate feedback should be presented at the earliest possible moment at each critical step of the learning process. *Feedback should,* therefore, be both *rapid* and *detailed.*

The more information an instructor receives about the degree to which trainees are learning what they are supposed to learn, the better he will be able to modify his own procedures in the direction of greater effectiveness and efficiency. The faster he receives this information, the sooner he can make these modifications.

These four constraints are external conditions of adequacy that must be achieved by a system design, no matter what else may be true of that design. For if these conditions are satisfied, experience has shown that learning efficiency improves substantially, *almost regardless of the content of the textual materials being employed.*

How PMI Fulfills the External Conditions of Adequacy

The reader of this book is by now redundantly aware of how these conditions of adequacy are met by Peer-Mediated Instruction. Students are provided with immediate and detailed feedback by their peers. States of mastery are established as prerequisites for progressing on to new material. Further, PMI systems are self-pacing in the sense that the attainment of a pre-established level of mastery by a given student is in no way whatever related to or dependent upon the attainment of this level by any other student. Finally, feedback to instructors is provided by the administrative sub-system of PMI/MS.

During the first meeting with the PMI Facilitators, I presented a history of PMI from its CAI origins through the New York Telephone application to illustrate how the aforementioned design criteria had been achieved in the past and how previously developed systems might serve as models for the development of a system in Jackson.

Issues Relating to Implementation

Subject Matter

The curricular focus of the Jackson Project was skill in reading, in particular, reading as it is defined implicitly by the test activities of national standardized tests, specifically activities dealing with knowledge of word meanings (*vocabulary*) and activities dealing with a certain kind of semantic paragraph processing (*comprehension*). (This focus certainly did not represent the total curricular policy of the Jackson Public Schools with regard to reading, but merely the short-term target of the PMI Project, which was to assist students with measurable deficiencies in these two skill areas.) As a design parameter, the mix of skills in the curriculum to be "peer mediated" would have to be a central consideration, especially, as in the current instance, where the activities necessitated by the practice of these skills are differently structured. Specifically, most text-based learning activities in vocabulary demand frequent and relatively simple responses from the student, simple in the sense of minimal opportunity for error. Thus, such vocabulary exercises are ideally suited for PMI adaptation. Since a student is so frequently called upon to deliver an answer, he can efficiently use the services of a peer to supervise his performance in the PMI mode. On the other hand, text-based activities for comprehension generally segment the student's time in such a manner that most of it is spent simply in reading. Thus, if a peer were assigned to that student as a PMI Teacher, he would spend most of his time doing nothing, in other words, a *prima facie* drop in the efficiency with which learning time is being used. Whatever the ultimate system design, it would have to cope with this fundamental difference between two classes of learning activities. The issue in particular was, assuming that optimal systems are designed for each skill separately, can the two be merged, and if not, what are the consequences?

(Margin notes:)

Reading to be defined as Vocabulary and Comprehension.

Systems differences between Vocabulary and Comprehension.

Texts

In my original proposal to the school people in Jackson, I suggested that we make use of materials of instruction that were already owned by the school system. As it turned out, a sufficient quantity of suitable materials was not immediately available. The purchase of new materials was thus necessitated, a circumstance of particular interest because of one terribly important fact of life about the economy of self-paced learning systems. One of the first things to be observed by the user of *good* self-paced instructional programs is the rapidity and voraciousness with which students charge through the materials. The *average* student in a self-paced program can be counted on to consume, in the same amount of learning time, three or four times more materials than does his lock-step counterpart. Thus, if a standard grade 3 book is given to a student in September to be used in a systematic self-paced mode, that student, as often as not, will need to be supplied with the grade 4 and 5 books before the end of the grade 3 year. The key design factor is this: In self-paced instruction, the flow of material to students must be continuous. And so it is clear that the costs of running a fully self-paced program on a classroom basis could be prohibitively expensive. Each classroom would require not one year's materials, but, practically speaking, many years' materials.

The solution adopted in Jackson was to conceptualize the program in terms of *learning centers*. A learning center is an ideal classroom used by groups of students in shifts. The economic difference between the learning center approach and conventional school organization is simply that in the latter students are assigned their own learning materials on a semi-permanent basis; in a learning center, students use materials on an as-needed basis. In the Jackson Project, four learning centers were to be established, each one serving four different classes during different hours of the day.

The necessity of a Learning Center design.

For the component of the program that would deal with reading comprehension, it was decided jointly to utilize basic SRA Reading Laboratories. There were two

Grade Level	Kit IIb	Kit IIc	Kit IIIa
2.5	Tan		
3.0	Brown	Tan	Orange
3.5	Red	Brown	Silver
4.0	Orange	Red	Olive
4.5	Gold	Orange	
5.0	Olive	Gold	Blue
5.5	Green	Olive	
6.0	Aqua	Green	Brown
7.0	Blue	Aqua	Green
8.0	Silver	Blue	Red
9.0		Silver	Tan
10.0			Gold
11.0			Aqua
12.0			

Figure 21. The distribution of grade level materials in three SRA Kits, by color code designation. (The levels in each kit are coded via color. Each level contains thirty reading passages.)

The selection of a Comprehension text. factors influencing the reasoning that went into this decision. First, the fact that performance improvement was to be measured by standardized tests necessitated a search for learning materials constructed in the same format, the same *medium,* if you will. The mediating structures of the learning activities for the SRA materials closely parallel those of the standardized tests. The second reason for selecting SRA was simply that this program provides a great deal of material at each grade level. You have, in remedial reading, the problem of needing to provide the student with a sufficient (for him) amount of material at a level of difficulty that allows the student to experience success before confronting more advanced material. The typical SRA kit provides thirty reading activities at each of six or more, one-half-grade incremented, instructional levels. Furthermore, the sequences in each kit overlap. Observe in Figure 21 the distribution in Kits II-b, II-c, and III-a, the kits used in Jackson. Notice that all three boxes contain materials at seven of the fourteen grade levels listed. Thus, for example, at grade level 3.5, a combination of three SRA kits would provide ninety reading passages at this grade level.

The problem of deciding which vocabulary materials to use was resolved with less deliberation. For one thing, there are few vocabulary programs suitable for remedial use that present a large enough number of words to justify the time spent learning them. Of these programs, only one recognized the deep importance of dealing with multiple word meanings or senses. This was a series of vocabulary workbooks published by EDL and called *Looking at Words in Sentences.* The EDL Workbook contained 25 or 30 lessons, each lesson containing among other things a dictionary-like presentation of five to ten words, with multiple meanings, and two sets of exercises, B and C, both of which comprehensively address the vocabulary items, their meanings, and various morphological characteristics. We used a five-book sequence, 140 lessons in all.

The selection of a Vocabulary text.

In addition to the SRA materials for comprehension and the EDL materials for vocabulary, we purchased a small inventory of programed decoding materials to use for cases of non-literacy.

Design of the System

From the very start of the design discussions, it was clear that vocabulary study activities and comprehension development activities could not be optimally served by a single classroom operating system; two were required, each with different sets of basic mechanics, what we came to call the Vocabulary sub-system and the Comprehension sub-system. The two sub-systems are unique and independent in the sense that a student may only engage in

The need for two sub-systems.

one sub-system at a time, for each sub-system itself makes total use of the student's time. At first, we did not believe it would be possible to run more than one of the sub-systems at the same time in the same classroom (presuming a subdivision into two functional groupings). On this point, experience has shown that we were wrong. It does seem practicable to manage the two functional groupings at the same time under a PMI/MS system. Once students fully master and internalize the operating procedures of the two sub-systems, both sub-systems probably can run in the same classroom and at the same time if this proves desirable in some instance.

System Elements Common to Both Sub-Systems
THE STUDY GUIDE

This is the student's *program,* his memory, his record of accomplishment, given to him as a checkpad to write in, to check off, and, hence, to record his progress and current state of accomplishment relative to pre-established goals.

Each student is supplied with a Study Guide, which is left in the classroom in a special file set up for that purpose—the Study Guide Box (see p. 134). Whenever, on a certain day, the PMI system is to operate, the student picks up his Study Guide, turns to that one of the two major sections that is to be used, and locates the spot where he left off the time before (in a manner to be described below).

THE UNIVERSAL AND NON-CONSUMABLE WASHABLE PLASTIC SCORING FORM

This scoring form is *universal* in that it provides one sub-form for use with vocabulary and another for use with comprehension (see Figure 22).

The use of the scoring form will be described shortly. There is an interesting feature of the scoring form quite aside from its use in scoring. In particular, the form is not paper, but styrene plastic, which can quickly be washed, dried, and re-used. That students seem to enjoy working with washable plastic paper is the least of the advantages. Foremost is the virtual elimination of the

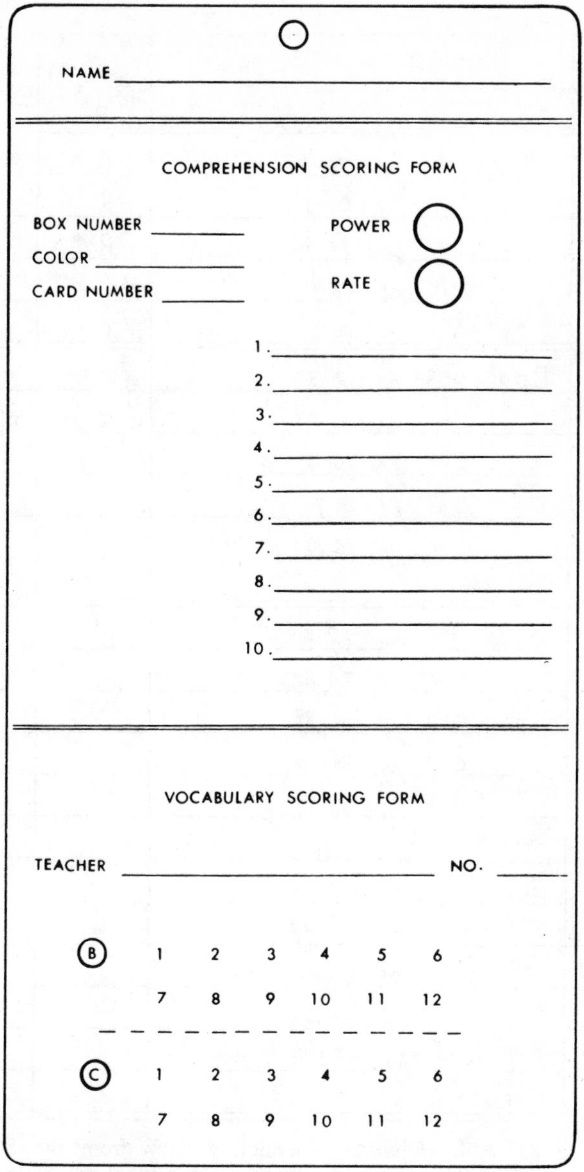

NAME ____________________

COMPREHENSION SCORING FORM

BOX NUMBER ________ POWER ◯

COLOR ________

CARD NUMBER ________ RATE ◯

1. ________
2. ________
3. ________
4. ________
5. ________
6. ________
7. ________
8. ________
9. ________
10. ________

VOCABULARY SCORING FORM

TEACHER ____________________ NO. ______

(B) 1 2 3 4 5 6

7 8 9 10 11 12

(C) 1 2 3 4 5 6

7 8 9 10 11 12

Figure 22. The face of the Scoring Form.

VOCABULARY FORM

SEQ. NO.	LOCATION	1	2
125	Book c-1 pp. 82, 83	PR	
126	c-1 pp. 86, 87	PR	
127	c-1 pp. 90, 91	PR	
128	c-1 pp. 94, 95	PR	
129	c-1 pp. 98, 99	dK	
	Test 130	dK	
131	Book c-2 pp. 2, 3	dK	
132	c-2 pp. 6, 7	dK	
133	c-2 pp. 10, 11		
134	c-2 pp. 14, 15		
135	c-2 pp. 18, 19		
	Test 136		
137	Book c-2 pp. 22, 23		
138	c-2 pp. 26, 27		
139	c-2 pp. 30, 31		
140	c-2 pp. 34, 35		
141	c-2 pp. 38, 39		
	Test 142		
143	Book c-2 pp. 42, 43		
144	c-2 pp. 46, 47-		
145	c-2 pp. 50, 51		
146	c-2 pp. 54, 55		
147	c-2 pp. 58, 59		
	Test 148		

Figure 23. A hypothetical Vocabulary Form from the Study
Guide. The initials are sign-offs from the Teacher (the peer).
This pupil as Student would start at 133.

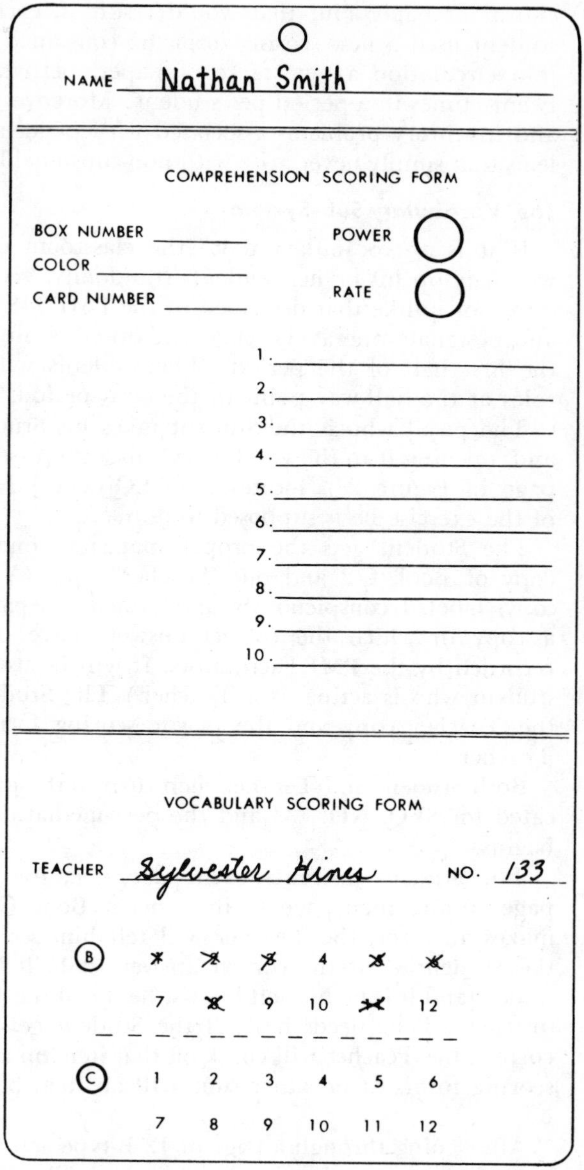

NAME Nathan Smith

COMPREHENSION SCORING FORM

BOX NUMBER ______ POWER ◯
COLOR ______
CARD NUMBER ______ RATE ◯

1. ______
2. ______
3. ______
4. ______
5. ______
6. ______
7. ______
8. ______
9. ______
10. ______

VOCABULARY SCORING FORM

TEACHER Sylvester Hines NO. 133

(B) ~~1~~ ~~2~~ ~~3~~ 4 ~~5~~ ~~6~~
7 ~~8~~ 9 10 ~~11~~ 12

(C) 1 2 3 4 5 6
7 8 9 10 11 12

Figure 24. Scoring form after one hypothetical pass.

enormous paper glut that would result if, each time a
student used a new scoring form, he consumed and put
into circulation a new piece of paper, perhaps ten to
twenty times in a period per student. Moreover, the cost
and inventory problems associated with paper are problems that simply never arise with non-consumable plastic.

The Vocabulary Sub-System

If it is a "vocabulary day," the classroom instructor
will pair up his or her students (randomly, via a procedure not unlike that described in the PMI/MS Manual)
and designate one as Teacher, the other as Student, for
the first half of the period. The students will reverse
roles at the half-way point in the class period.

The pupil who is the Student takes his Study Guide
and, opening it to the vocabulary sub-section (see sample
page in Figure 23), locates the SEQ[uence] NO[mber]
of the exercise he is supposed to do next.

The Student gets the proper materials, one Stutent
copy of Book C-2 and one Teacher copy. (A Teacher
copy, labeled conspicuously and attached separately, is
a copy in which the correct answers have been pre-
recorded by the PMI Facilitators. It will be used by the
student who is acting as a Teacher.) The Student gives
the Teacher copy and the plastic scoring form to the
Teacher.

Both Student and Teacher then turn to the pages indicated for SEQ. NO. 133 and the peer-mediation process
begins.

The Student processes each page, e.g., for 133, first
page 10 and then page 11 in Teacher Book C-2. If he
makes an error, the Teacher will tell him so; he'll tell
the Student what the correct answer is; he'll help him
understand it if he himself knows; he'll call the classroom
instructor if he needs help. If the Student gets an item
correct, the Teacher will check off that item on the plastic
scoring form. At no other time will an item be checked
off.

After going through a page of 12 B-type activities, one
at a time, the scoring form might look like Figure 24.
Had all of the items been checked off, this would mean

that the Student had gotten them all right. The un-marked items represent exercise items to which a repeat exposure is justified. And so, the Teacher has the Student go back to the first item missed, in this case item 4, and start again, but this time doing just the items that have not been checked, i.e., 4, 7, 9, 10, and 12. After this, another inspection reveals that the second pass has brought the scoring form closer to completion (see Figure 25). On the third pass, the Teacher has the Student do just items 4 and 9, and so on, until the Teacher has been able to check off every item.

When this process is completed, the two proceed to the C activity on page 11 and work through it in the same way. When both the B and C exercises are completed, the Teacher certifies this accomplishment by signing his initials in the Student's Study Guide, in the appropriate place.

The Vocabulary Form in the Study Guide has a Student proceed through five lessons in sequence in the EDL workbook, e.g., SEQ. NOS. 131-135. SEQ. NO. 136, you will observe, is a Test, a short ten-item test on the words presented in the preceding five lessons. The Vocabulary Form format embodies the plan that if a Student passes the five-lesson test, he is permitted to go on to the next block of material. If he has not performed satisfactorily, he must go through the five lessons once again under the guidance of a Teacher (hence the column marked "2" on the Vocabulary Form). The passing threshold was set at 8 out of 10 correct. We are finding, as the system is in active operation, that numerous contingency designs are possible.

(One of the problems that always must be faced is that the external criterion of *insistence on mastery* is an ideal that never can be fully met in learning situations. The dynamic is a simple one. Given a specific list of exercise items, the more a student has mastered, the fewer exercise items are remaining to master productively. Thus, at a certain point, it becomes more efficient of a student's time to expose him to an entirely new block of items, perhaps the next block in sequence. No learning system could work if it insisted that every student learn every-

Not every student will learn everything.

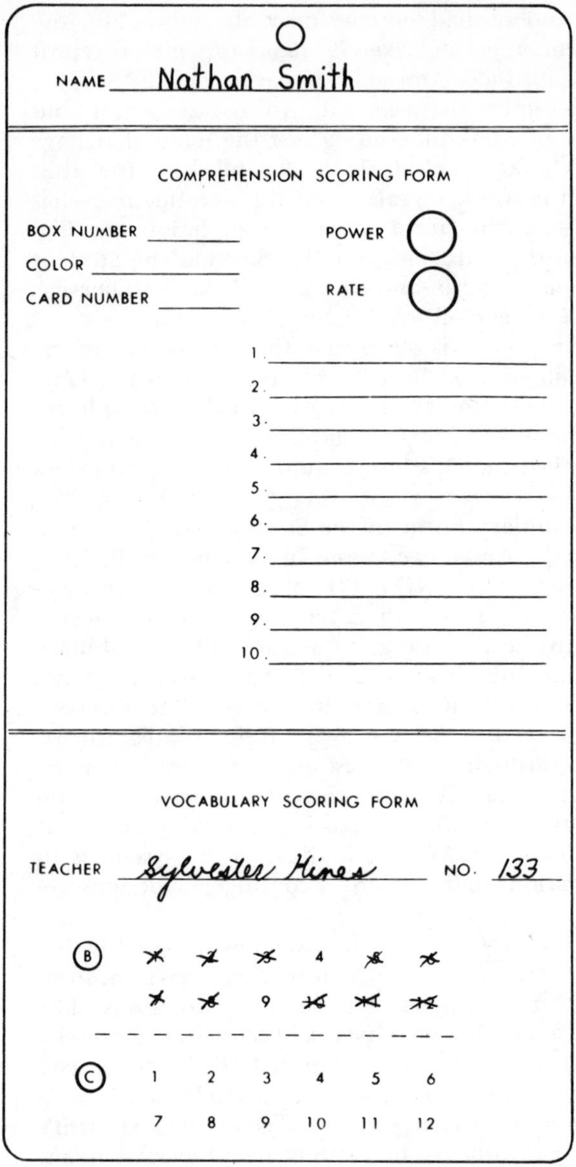

COMPREHENSION SCORING FORM

NAME Nathan Smith

BOX NUMBER _____   POWER ◯
COLOR _____
CARD NUMBER _____   RATE ◯

1. _____
2. _____
3. _____
4. _____
5. _____
6. _____
7. _____
8. _____
9. _____
10. _____

VOCABULARY SCORING FORM

TEACHER Sylvester Hines   NO. 133

Ⓑ 1 2 3 4 5 6
   7 8 9 10 11 12

Ⓒ 1 2 3 4 5 6
   7 8 9 10 11 12

Figure 25. The same scoring form after a second pass through the list, re-doing the unmarked items.

thing in some fixed period of time. The best that can be achieved is that available time will be used with maximal efficiency. Requiring a student to learn everything surely gets to be a proposition of diminishing returns. Thus, one of the most consequential and complex decisions that has to be made is the establishment of reasonable criteria of mastery as performance goals. In actuality, performance thresholds for mastery serve best in a prescription function that assigns differential amounts or types of work.)

If the period ends or if the half-way point arrives while a Student is in the middle of a lesson, the Student merely takes back his scoring form and his Study Guide. Next time, when again he is a Student, he will simply hand his scoring form and his Study Guide to his new Teacher. The new Teacher will start the Student on the first unchecked item. Whenever a Student finishes a lesson, i.e., a B and C activity, the Teacher simply wipes the form clean with a sponge, dries it, and starts on the next lesson, or administers a test, as the case will be after every five lessons.

A record of student progress is kept by the classroom instructor, who records progress on the Vocabulary page of the Master Log, a sample of which appears in Figure 26. Every so often, perhaps once or twice a week, the instructor goes through each student's Study Guide, looking to see the last test completed. The instructor enters this information into the Master Log, thus constructing a bar graph of student progress through the vocabulary syllabus.

The Comprehension Sub-System

On a "comprehension day," students *do not* pair off with one another; they merely collect their Study Guides and take their seats. The classroom instructor selects two or three students to be "checkers-for-the-day." (The effective student-checker ratio seems to range from 8:1 to 12:1.) These checkers take positions at special desks, where they will have before them the Correct Answer cards from all of the SRA kits. Students, on the other hand, open their Study Guides to the comprehension

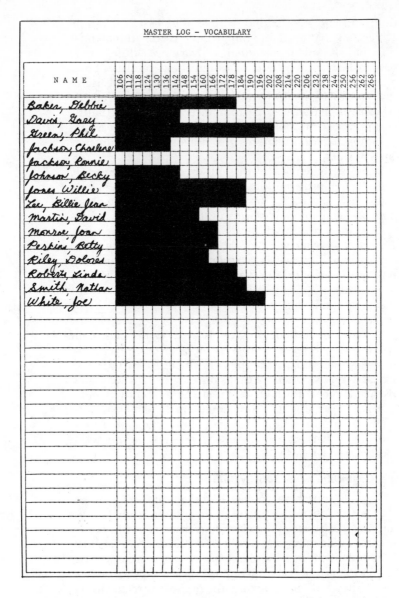

Figure 26. A sample Master Log Vocabulary page from the Jackson Project.

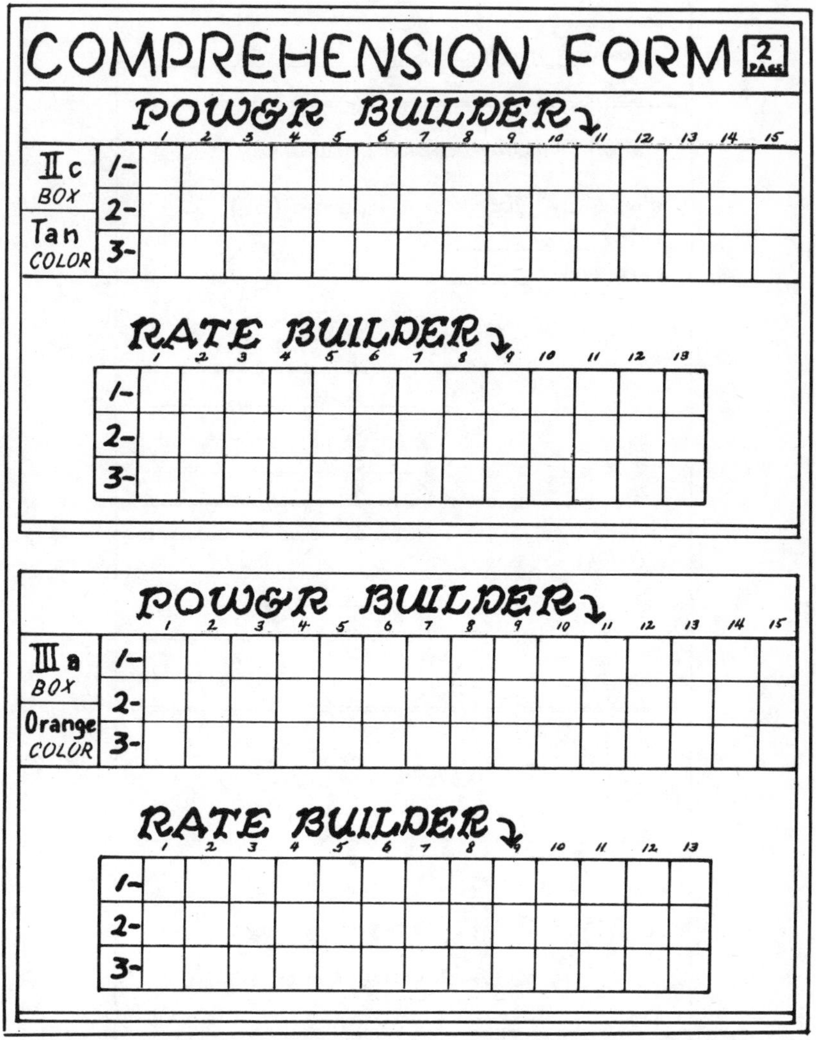

COMPREHENSION FORM 2 PAGE

POWER BUILDER

		1	2	3	4	5	6	7	8	9	10	11	12	13	14	15
IIc BOX	1-															
	2-															
Tan COLOR	3-															

RATE BUILDER

	1	2	3	4	5	6	7	8	9	10	11	12	13
1-													
2-													
3-													

POWER BUILDER

		1	2	3	4	5	6	7	8	9	10	11	12	13	14	15
IIIa BOX	1-															
	2-															
Orange COLOR	3-															

RATE BUILDER

	1	2	3	4	5	6	7	8	9	10	11	12	13
1-													
2-													
3-													

Figure 27. Page 2 of the 15-page Comprehension section of the Study Guide. This page contains check-charts for color level Tan in Kit IIc and color level Orange in Kit IIIa.

NAME Nathan Smith

COMPREHENSION SCORING FORM

BOX NUMBER IIc POWER (X)

COLOR Tan

CARD NUMBER 6 RATE ( )

1. a
2. b
3. b
4. a
5. c
6. a
7.
8.
9.
10.

VOCABULARY SCORING FORM

TEACHER ______ NO. ______

(B) 1 2 3 4 5 6
7 8 9 10 11 12

(C) 1 2 3 4 5 6
7 8 9 10 11 12

Figure 28. A scoring form as it might look after Power Builder Card 6 in Tan IIc has been read and processed by Nathan Smith.

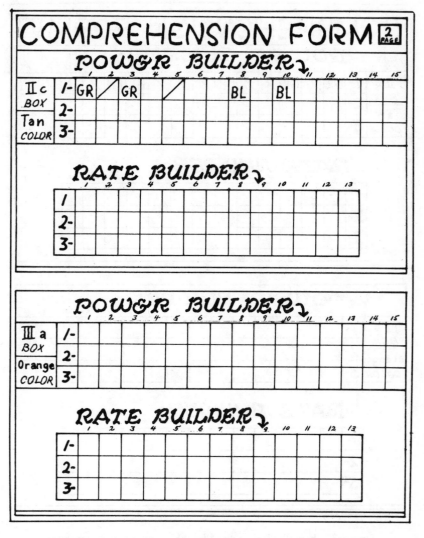

Figure 29. Page 2 as it might look after a student has completed
six reading selections.

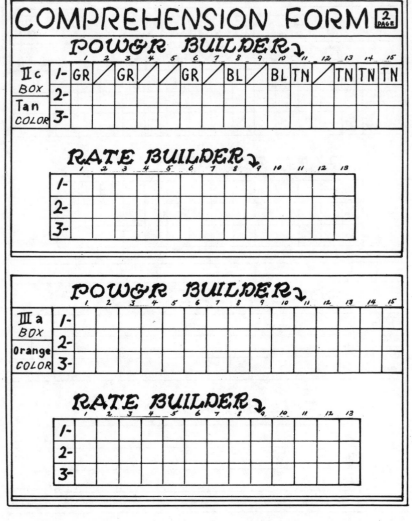

Figure 30. Hypothetical status after the student has completed all 15 reading selections. More reading is called for. Cards 2, 4, 5, 7, 9, and 12 are available for re-reading

section and find their places. There are 15 pages in this
section, each containing two check-charts for two sequential levels of SRA materials. There are, then, 30 ordered
check-charts, one for each color level of the three SRA
kits presented in Figure 20.

Let us examine one of these check-charts (see Figure
27). Imagine that you are a student about to start work
on level Tan in IIc and that the check-chart for it is
clean. Your job is establishing reading mastery by performing well on 12 of the 15 numbered Power Builder
selections and 11 of the 13 numbered Rate Builder selections. The procedure you follow is this: Select any reading passage card you choose from the designated box
and color. Study the comprehension questions at the end
of the passage, read the passage, and write the answers
to the questions on the plastic scoring form (see Figure
28). Now take the plastic scoring form, along with your
Study Guide, to a "checker," who will check your work
on the spot against the Correct Answers. If you have
made no more than one error (the threshold established
at the beginning of the program), the "checker" will
initial the corresponding box in the Study Guide. If you
make more than one mistake, the checker will put a line
through the box to remind you that this passage is available for re-reading if re-reading is necessary. You then
study your errors, if you wish, and then wash off your
scoring form. After reading six selections, your check-
chart might look like Figure 29.

As you go through the selections on Line 1, keep track
of how many boxes you have received initials in. Whenever this number reaches 12, you stop, even if you have
read only 12 (i.e., performed successfully on every card).
If, having read all 15, you have not yet received initials
in 12, as in Figure 30, you start with Line 2, now for the
first time re-reading passages you have read before, but
only those passages that have not previously been initialed, e.g., cards 2, 4, 5, 7, 9, and 12 in Figure 30.

If, on this second pass, three of the six uninitialed
columns receive initials, the student has completed the
Power Builder section. If 12 columns are still not initialed at the end of the second pass, the student goes on

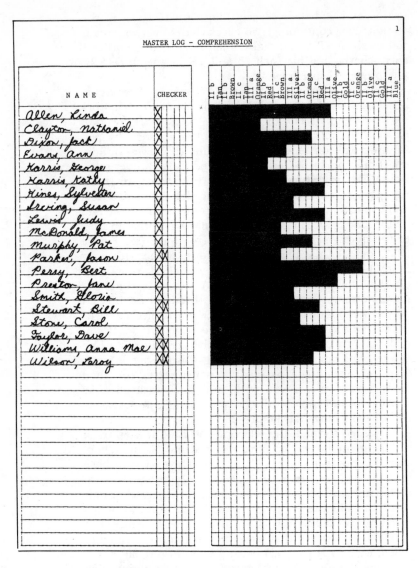

Figure 31. A sample page 1 of the Master Log Comprehension
sections from the Jackson Project.

to Pass 3, and finally is automatically exempted, although the Jackson experience shows that the third pass is infrequently used.

Progress through the Comprehension sub-system is recorded by the classroom instructor in the two-page Comprehension section of the Master Log (see Figure 31). Each column in the right-hand matrix is labeled for a color level in the composite sequence of the three SRA kits listed in Figure 20. The "checker" columns were provided so instructors could keep track of checker assignments.

Work Performed by the PMI Facilitators

The system was designed jointly by myself and the PMI Facilitators, but the Facilitators themselves carried out in its entirety the assembly of the system for each of their schools. This task included the following:

1. Designing the formats and laying out the syllabus sequence for the Study Guides and seeing that the Study Guides were printed.
2. Marking correct answers in the Teacher versions of the EDL workbooks.
3. Designing and printing all supporting materials, e.g., the Master Logs, instruction sheets for instructors, tests, etc.
4. Purchasing materials.
5. Installing the entire system in the four learning centers.
6. Participating in the orientation of classroom instructors and the supervision of operations.

The Orientation of Classroom Instructors

The orientation of instructors was carried out in $1\frac{1}{2}$ days, beginning in the afternoon and going through the next day.

COMPREHENSION SUB-SYSTEM

Administrative Procedures

1. Take answer cards (in their boxes) from SRA kits and place where "checkers" will use them.
2. At beginning of period, appoint one checker for each 15 students. This number may have to be increased to one checker for 10 students.

Student Procedures

1. Work on one color level at a time.
2. Select SRA cards in any available order, but *across a line,* not down a column.
3. Work until 12 Power Builder columns and 11 Rate Builder columns have been initialed.
4. Do not start a new "pass" in either the Power Builder or Rate Builder until all columns have been initialed or "lined" by the checker.
5. Process an SRA card:
   a) study the "How Well Did You Read" questions
   b) read the passage
   c) answer the "How Well Did You Read" questions on the Comprehension Scoring Form
   d) return the card to its appropriate place
   e) present the Comprehension Scoring Form along with Study Guide to the checker.

Checker Procedures

1. Take out the answer card for the assignment just done by the student.
2. Compare card with student's Comprehension Scoring Form.
3. If student makes *no more than* one error, initial the appropriate box on his Study Guide; if more than one error, put a line through this box.
4. Return Study Guide; erase Scoring Form (or throw away if paper form used).
5. Put answer card back.

Figure 32. The orientation hand-out to classroom instructors reviewing the Comprehension Sub-System that had just been simulated.

1. *First Afternoon*
      Presentation of the Project rationale
      Presentation of PMI rationale
      Verbal description of system components and operation
2. *First Morning*
      Simulation of Comprehension Sub-System with instructors in Student and "checker" roles
      Review (See Figure 32)
      Simulation of Vocabulary Sub-System with instructors in Teacher and Student roles
      Review (See Figure 33)
3. *Second Afternoon*
      Review start-up schedule and procedures
      Review relations between Facilitators and instructors
      Question-and-Answer period
      Rap
      Farewell

Costs of Basic Texts

The materials cost to equip a Learning Center according to the inventory in Figure 34 is approximately $450. Each Learning Center will service six classes per day of 30 students each, or 180 students per day. The materials are non-consumable and so, if one reasons that the materials will last four years, the same set of materials will service 720 students over four years at a cost of slightly less than 70¢ per student, a figure that places this kind of PMI system well within the range of the normal expenditure for materials.

PMI is cheap!

Concluding Remark

The Jackson PMI Project represents an important landmark in my own thinking. Both the P.S. 129 and New York Telephone projects had been carried out under the very close supervision and management of myself and other members of the research staff. Thus, even though both projects were successful, the question always re-

VOCABULARY SUB-SYSTEM

Administrative Procedures

1. Pair students at beginning of class.
2. Set timer to ring at halfway point in class.
3. Make first-half Teacher-Student designation.

Student Procedures

1. Start with first unchecked sequence number (Seq. No.) in Study Guide.
2. Get Student and Teacher versions of text, giving Teacher version to the Teacher.
3. Give Teacher your plastic Scoring Form (or paper).
4. Study as long as necessary.
5. Do Ⓑ exercises out loud to Teacher one at a time until Teacher acknowledges completion.
6. Do Ⓒ exercises in the same manner.
7. Go on to next Sequence Number.
8. Reverse roles when the bell rings.
9. Replace plastic Scoring Form in your Study Guide.

Teacher Procedures

1. Fill out Scoring Form (your name).
2. Correct Ⓑ exercises.
   a) If Student makes an error, tell him the correct answer. Go to next item.
   b) If Student gets it right, tell him so and cross off the number of that item on the Scoring Form. Go to next item.

  c) At end of B exercises, if uncrossed-off items remain on Scoring Form, take Student on another "pass," having him do just the unscored items. Follow "a" and "b" above. Keep going through B until all items have been checked off.

3. Correct C exercises (same procedures as B exercises).

4. When B and C are completed, place your initials in the appropriate box in the Student's Study Guide.

Vocabulary Test Procedures

1. When Student comes to a Test,

  a) Teacher gets test (identified by sequence number on test folder) from the Vocabulary Test file *and* test answer form from stack, and gives both to Student.

  b) Student takes test with no assistance from Teacher.

  c) Teacher gets correct answer from file and corrects.

  d) If test has two errors or less, Teacher initials Student's Study Guide and Student is permitted to go on to next block of sequence numbers.

  e) If more than two errors, Teacher "lines" test box in Study Guide. Student must re-do block of sequence numbers.

  f) Teacher returns test form and answer sheet to file and gives Student's answer form to class instructor.

Figure 33. The hand-out review of the Vocabulary Sub-System.

Jackson PMI Project

TEXTS:
  EDL c-1 "teacher" and "student" copies
  EDL c-2 "teacher" and "student" copies
  EDL d   "teacher" and "student" copies
  EDL e   "teacher" and "student" copies
  EDL f   "teacher" and "student" copies
  SRA II-b
  SRA II-c
  SRA III-a
  BRL Decoding Programed Textbooks "teacher" and
  "student" copies

SYSTEM COMPONENTS:
  Study Guides, one for each pupil
  Study Guide Box, one for each class
  Universal Plastic Scoring Form, one for each pupil
  Vocabulary Tests, 4 copies of each for each class-
  room
  Vocabulary Test Answer Keys, one for each copy
  of the test
  Vocabulary Test Answer Forms, a bundle
  Vocabulary Test File, to hold Tests and Answer
  Keys
  Master Log, one for each class
  Nylon Tip pens, 60 for each classroom (30 as spares)
  Sponges, 20 for each classroom
  Timer (no wall clocks available)
  Dish, one for each classroom (to hold water for
  sponges)

Figure 34. Classroom inventory for the Jackson PMI Project.

mained as to the portion of that success that could be attributed to the management of well-wishers. But the Jackson Project was managed, and managed superbly well, by the in-service staff itself and especially by the three PMI Facilitators. In other words, here, in Jackson, the school staff showed it could handle PMI on its own.

What follows is my letter to the Superintendent of Instruction summarizing the then current status of the Jackson PMI Project.

June 14, 1972

Dr. Brandon Sparkman
Superintendent of Instruction
Jackson Public Schools
P.O. Box 2338
Jackson, Mississippi 39205

Dear Dr. Sparkman:

The purpose of this letter is to provide you with an informal analysis of the quantitative results of the Jackson PMI Project. At the outset, I must state that this analysis should be viewed more as suggestive than as definitive, for several reasons. In the first place, the Project itself was conducted as a feasibility study and not as a carefully controlled comparative study of contrasting methodologies. This means in particular that any effects observed are open to numerous explanations. Before the precise contribution of the PMI experience to these effects can be ascertained, either existing data will have to be subjected to much more precise scrutiny than my resources currently allow or, and more probably, your staff would have to re-run the PMI system according to a much more rigorous experimental design, which is precisely what our discussions have led me to believe is your intention. Secondly, I myself can scarcely be counted as an independent and unbiased evaluator, inasmuch as the Project was carried out under my direction, indirect though that direction may have been. In fairness to this analysis, however, I should point out that the testing procedures were designed and implemented under the supervision of the Jackson Public Schools and I am aware of no irregularities or improprieties associated with the execution of these procedures.

I would like to begin with a review of the salient circumstances under which the Project was originally planned so that the structure of my analysis can be **Review of** placed in perspective. The Planning Staff included Miss **project** Margaret Allen and Mrs. Helen Power of the In-Service **planning.** Office and Mrs. Charlene Sharman (Powell School), Mrs. Posey Smith (Callaway School), and Mrs. Rosa Twyner (Peeples School), and me. In the initial meeting of the Staff, it became clear that the mechanics of any truly adequate experimental design would have been so time-consuming as to preclude classroom operations of PMI during the Spring term. The Staff decided that it would be better to run the PMI system as soon as possible, gathering whatever data could be gathered, than to postpone the use of the system until the Fall term of 1972. Funding, staffing, the urgency of the instructional purposes for which PMI was being used in the first place, the fact that the effects of PMI have frequently been large enough to observe even with gross performance statistics —these and other factors were involved in the decision.

The Staff concluded that it would be possible to administer pre- and posttests to the PMI classes and in **Use of** particular that two sets of such tests should be given. The **standardized** first set was to consist of two different forms of a national **and** standardized test. The second was to contain two differ- **"home-made"** ent forms of a "home-made" test based upon the content **tests.** of the texts being used, *but* cast in a format identical to the national standardized test. A word of explanation is called for here. The Staff felt that an assessment based upon a national standardized test would be of greater value to the Jackson Public Schools than would be a home-made test. On the other hand, there was considerable doubt that the effects of PMI would show up on a standardized test. For one thing, we could not know without detailed study the extent to which such a national test was a reliable test of whatever it was that the texts we were going to use actually taught. For another, we knew that even under the best possible circumstances, we could count on no more than twenty hours of instruction in Vocabulary and twenty hours of instruction in Comprehension before the end of the school year. Indeed, the student average has proved to be less than that, sometimes substantially less. Thus, even if the text materials and the tests were indeed compatible, students simply might not receive a sufficient amount of instruction for measurable differences to be observed. (Recall that a grade level increase of 1.9 in Vocabulary was recorded in the New York Telephone study after fifty hours of instruction, in contrast to the projected twenty in Jackson.) For these reasons, we decided to develop a test that would explicitly cover just the material we were trying to teach, on the assumption that if PMI were teaching this material effectively, our test would reflect such improvement. I will have little more to say about the home-made test because, in fact, we did record gains on the national test as well as on the home-made test. But I hasten to re-make what I consider to be a central fact in the interpretation of the national test results: They are achieved in something less than forty instructional hours, twenty for Vocabulary and twenty for Comprehension.

The national standardized test that we used was the Nelson Test. We selected this test because it is widely used to measure reading "age" in terms of grade level equivalents, because of its range of reliability (roughly third grade to tenth grade), and because the subject students in the three schools were thought to have reading ages that would fall within this range. I must point out in this connection that we had no way of knowing in advance of the pretest exactly or even roughly what the current reading age of the subject students was, for very little current data existed. As will be noted below, the Nelson Test was an unfortunate choice in several instances because of the relatively advanced reading age of a number of students. In particular, there can be little doubt that the magnitude of certain performance differences has been artificially suppressed by a "ceiling effect."

Problems of test selection.

Finally, the Jackson PMI system was planned to run

Table 7. Distribution of students in the Jackson Project.

Grade Level	School	Number of Students
7	Peeples	48
8	Peeples	49
9	Powell	82
11/12	Callaway	73

in three different schools with four classes in each school experiencing PMI, and at four different grade levels. Subject students were distributed as indicated in Table 7; Number of Students refers only to those for whom we were able to collect a complete set of scores.

Table 8 shows the *magnitude of the performance increase,* as measured by the Nelson Test and stated as grade level equivalents, for each of the four grades tested on Vocabulary (Vocab.) and Paragraph Comprehension (Comp.). Keeping in mind that I have no certainty about the extent to which PMI is causal in these increments, note that one grade level (1.0) of difference on the Nelson Test is what one might expect to observe after ten months of conventional instruction (i.e., one full school year). The values recorded in Table 8 for Vocabulary and Comprehension were generated in *one month* (or less) of PMI exposure for each sub-skill. It is hard to be disappointed with such performance. Figures 35 through 38 show pre- and posttest means stated as grade level equivalents (from the Nelson Test) for each grade.

When the Project was being planned, the Planning Staff recognized that a certain portion of any observed

Table 8. Performance increase in grade equivalents.

Apparent performance improvements

Grade Level	N	Vocab.	Comp.	Combined
7	48	1.1	1.4	1.1
8	49	1.5	2.2	2.0
9	82	.9	1.4	1.0
11/12	73	1.0	1.0	1.0

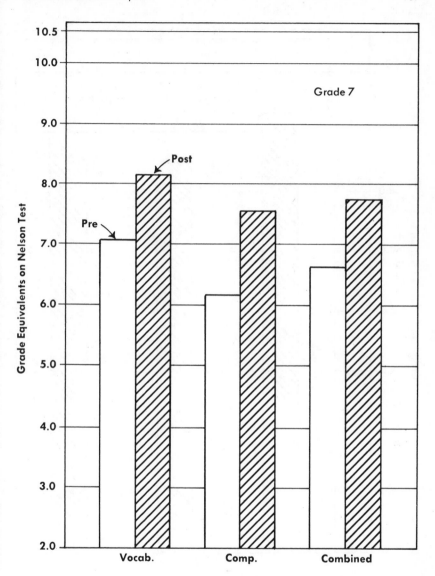

Figure 35. Pre- and Posttest Means, Grade 7, Jackson Project.
(N=48)

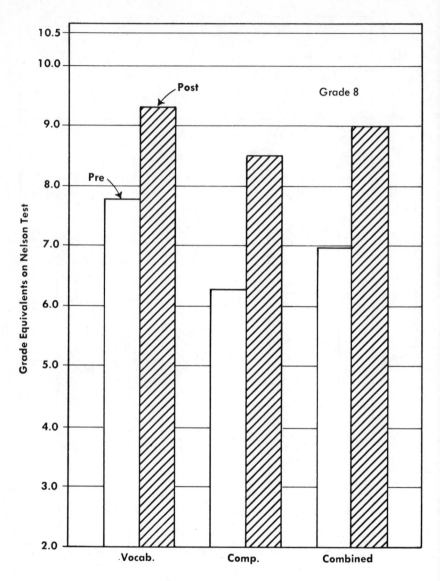

Figure 36. Pre- and Posttest Means, Grade 8, Jackson Project.
(N=49)

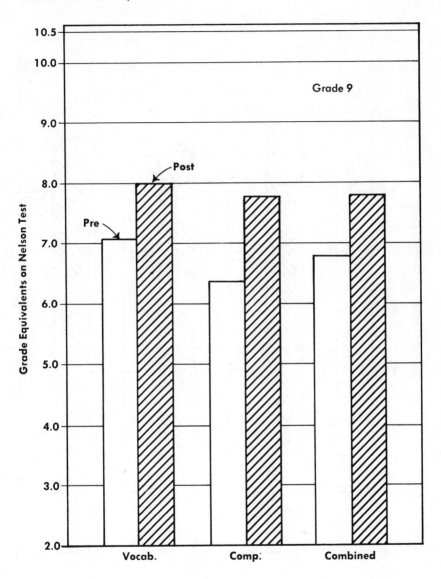

Figure 37. Pre- and Posttest Means, Grade 9, Jackson Project.
(N = 60)

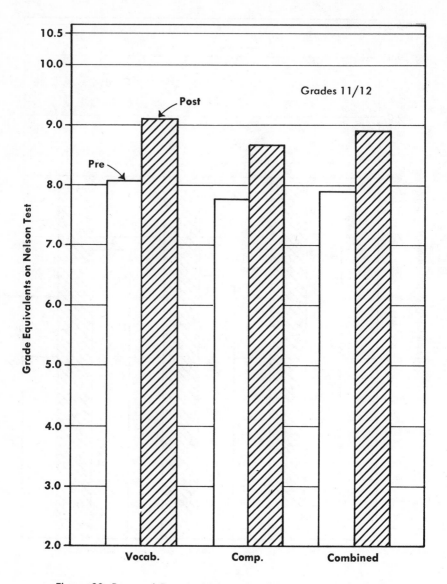

Figure 38. Pre- and Posttest Means, Grades 11 and 12, Jackson
Project.
(N=73)

performance increments would have to be attributed to *the fact* of being in school for two months (i.e., the approximate duration of the PMI Project). In order to get some idea of just how much growth might have been attributable simply to the school experience, we selected at random a second sample of students, who would not be experiencing PMI, and we administered to them, at the same time as the PMI students, pre- and posttests. (This second sample can only in the remotest sense be thought of as a control group, for, as it turned out, there were great differences in initial ability between the two groups. In two grades, these differences were 2.5 grade levels; in a third, the difference was more than one grade level. I reiterate that this situation could not have been controlled if PMI was to be operational immediately because the reading age of the students we were to be working with could not be known until they actually took the pretest.) On the average, students in the second sample increased their reading age by .5, apparently independently of their grade in school. This improvement was observed "across the board." This increase may seem surprisingly high until one reflects on two facts: first, that these students were themselves experiencing instruction (apparently of high quality) over the same period of time as the PMI students were experiencing PMI; and second, that in taking a test the first time, students generally learn things about the test that will later enable them to perform better on a different version of the same test independent of any learning that may have taken place in the interim. More to the point, in my opinion, is simply to recognize that the increments reported for the PMI students, which are more than double those for the second group of students, contain components that have nothing to do with the PMI treatment *per se*.

The problem of experimental control.

A constraint on interpretation.

In addition to the pre- and posttest comparisons, we made an assessment of the PMI program in terms of the views of the classroom teachers who volunteered for or were assigned to PMI classes. These teachers were asked to respond to a questionnaire in confidence. Ten of the twelve teachers responded; these responses are tabulated

Instructor assessment.

The making of a questionnaire is always difficult because it involves making assumptions about what is important. Were I to formulate the questions, they would, for better or worse, reflect my own biases about what you ought to consider important in the assessment of the PMI instructional system. But, the relevance of criteria for evaluating instructional systems in your classrooms is something that obviously you can judge better than I, for you are "on the scene," doing the job. Recognizing this, I did not make up this questionnaire myself; I solicited questions for the questionnaire from the PMI Facilitators, Mrs. Posey Smith, Mrs. Charlene Sharman, and Mrs. Rosa Twyner. My contribution has merely been to adapt and format these questions for the sake of consistency. I accept full responsibility for any distortions that may have arisen in the editing process.

Do not write your name on the questionnaire. And please be completely frank in expressing your opinions. Do not consult with any other instructor in the PMI program.

When you have completed the questionnaire, please place it in the attached envelop and mail it. None of the questionnaires will be opened until all twelve (one from each participating teacher) have been received.

Peter S. Rosenbaum
Teachers College, Columbia University
May 1, 1972

Figure 39. PMI Questionnaire for Classroom Instructors.

Part A Check one column for each numbered item.

	yes	neutral	no
1. Do you feel that PMI is an important innovation in instruction relative to other things called "innovations in instruction?"	9	1	0
2. Do you believe that students can learn on a more individual basis in a peer-mediated situation than in a normal teaching situation?	7	2	0
3. Do you feel that the PMI program is generally effective in the area of Vocabulary?	7	1	1
4. Do you feel that the PMI program is generally effective in the area of Comprehension?	9	0	0
5. Do you find PMI to be a well-organized classroom activity?	10	0	0
6. Do students tend to be positively motivated toward the PMI system?	7	3	0
7. Do you feel that the tasks of PMI teaching (that is, acting in the Teacher role) provide reassurance and confidence for weaker students?	9	1	0
8. Does the relationship that develops between pairs of students working in the Teacher-Student relationship appear to be mutually rewarding?	—	—	—
9. Do you think that the interpersonal aspect of PMI contributes to the students' becoming effective adults?	6	4	0
10. Under PMI, does a student seem to feel that his performance is appreciated and that the results of his work are significant?	8	2	0
11. Do you feel that the self-pacing aspect of PMI eliminates certain basic sources of frustration for students?	9	0	1

(Continued on following page)

12. Do you think that the effectiveness of PMI is independent of social background?	7	3	0
13. Would you feel comfortable in calling PMI an *individualized learning program?*	7	3	0
14. Was sufficient orientation provided to you by your PMI Facilitator and Dr. Rosenbaum?	10	0	0
15. Has your PMI Facilitator served you adequately? (Please write suggested improvements on the back of this sheet.)	7	2	0
16. Do you now, having once worked with PMI, feel confident that you could run the PMI system with minimal support from your Facilitator?	8	2	0
17. Do you feel that you could now do a good job as a Facilitator yourself?	4	5	1
18. Would it in any way be an inconvenience to you to manage more than one PMI class per day?	2	1	7
19. Would you want to see the PMI system run again next Fall?	9	1	0

Figure 39 (continued).

in Figure 39. In certain cases, the number of responses does not add up to ten because not all teachers answered all questions. Also, question 8 in Part A has not been tabulated because of the number of comments regarding the ambiguity of the wording.

On the strength of these findings, I should like to think that you would consider PMI to number among those of your current projects that are rated as promising. I understand that it is currently your intention to expand the number of PMI Learning Centers from four to twelve. I believe that the data reported herein support this decision.

Preliminary findings are suggestive of positive effect and acceptance.

Part B   Fill in B (for "better") in one of the two columns
for each lettered item. Leave blank to signify "no
noticeable change."

	before PMI	*with PMI*
a. Students' attitude toward classroom work	2	7
b. Students' work habits	1	7
c. Students' interest in classroom business	1	8
d. Students' attitude toward you	—	3
e. Students' attitude toward each other	—	7
f. Students' ability to work under self-direction	1	8
g. Discipline	—	6
h. Attendance	2	2

The PMI system developed in Jackson is, as I am sure
you are aware, fully capable of standing on its own two
feet without further assistance from me. Still, I have
numerous suggestions to make regarding the structure
of use for PMI next Fall, regarding the utilization of
trained staff, and regarding further measurements that
you are likely to want to make. I would be happy to
discuss these with you at your convenience.

In closing, I would like to say to you that working with
the staff of the Jackson Public Schools has been one of
the most pleasurable experiences of my professional life.
I have been struck by your competence, by your dedication, and by your teamwork. I must tell you that the
Jackson Project is the first major PMI project for which
I have not provided personal direct supervision, in the
sense of on-site availability. Although it is true that future use of PMI in your schools and others will increasingly make clear that PMI systems are dependably easy to
implement, there was no such certainty in my mind when
the Project began. And for this reason I must offer my
special commendation to the three Reading Facilitators,
Mrs. Sharman, Mrs. Smith, and Mrs. Twyner, for a

superb performance conducted with great vigor, great dedication, and great professionalism. I have no reservation whatever about their ability to supervise and direct the extension of PMI methodology in whatever directions may seem appropriate.

I am at your disposal to discuss the details of this analysis or any other matter relating to the Jackson PMI Project.

> Very truly yours,
> Peter S. Rosenbaum
> Associate Professor of
>   Linguistics and Education
> Teachers College, Columbia
>   University

6

Observations and Reflections

Learning occurs for both participants in the PMI dyad.

As the reader may appreciate, my earliest understanding of Peer-Mediated Instruction pictured the Teacher in the PMI dyad as a computer simulator, for, at the time, the Teacher executed procedures on analogy to those executed by the computer in IBM's drill-and-practice CAI programs. I gave little attention to the issue of whether the Teacher would learn anything; indeed, I was willing to accept that the Teacher might learn nothing at all. For inasmuch as the time spent by that pupil as a Student in the dyad was likely to prove so very productive, or so I had reason to hope, I was willing to see half of that pupil's time devoted to an activity, namely Teaching, from which no educationally useful outcome might be derived. On balance, I believed, the pupil would still come out far ahead.

Almost from the first, however, classroom teachers with whom I was working advised me that pupils would also learn while performing as Teachers. And too, the home-spun wisdom that "there is no better way to learn something than to teach it" frequently cropped up in discussions. Of course the classroom teachers were right. Not only do Students learn, Teachers learn also. The choice of terms for the roles of the dyad, "Teacher" and "Student," turn out to be quite unfortunate because of the connotations that attach to the words "teacher" and "student"; they generally conjure the idea of someone who *knows* transmitting and imprinting what he knows upon someone who doesn't. But in a PMI system, these terms simply identify different, although interwoven, acts; *all of these acts,* whether Teacher initiated or Student initiated, address the course content as it exists in the materials of instruction. For example, in the spelling prototype of PMI described in Chapter Two, Students *listened* to words and *wrote* them, but Teachers *read* them, *spoke* them, and *analyzed* them for errors. And since roles were systematically swapped, all pupils engaged in all five of these modalities. Without some research, it would be speculation as to the relative contributions of being a Teacher as opposed to being a Student to the total sum learned. But it would be foolish, by the same token, to assume that the contribution made through Teaching would prove less than substantial.

In any case, a probable cause for the apparent potency of PMI is the simple fact that the two roles, Teacher and Student, force a multi-mode engagement with the subject matter in such intensity as has not heretofore been achievable under conventional classroom communication structures.

Materials of instruction are consumed at a very fast rate.

In the typical instructional setting, the classroom teacher controls the rate at which pupils can progress through a given body of instructional materials. Largely as a consequence of this fact, the content of most textual materials of instruction is organized in blocks that correspond to units in the school calendar, usually weeks; one week on Lesson 21, the next on Lesson 22, and so forth. Most of the major grade school spelling texts, for example, are structured into 36 lessons; * the classroom

---

* It is quite likely that the notions of a 36-lesson structure and self-pacing are not incompatible. And if they are not, this structure surely would be a desirable feature in spelling texts, for such a text would serve schools well in the transition from lock-step to self-pacing methodology.

teacher is meant to cover one lesson per week throughout the school year. (The concession sometimes made to individual differences in ability in such texts is the ploy of incorporating supplementary—sometimes called "bonus" —words in each lesson for "better spellers," a euphemism for the students who already can spell most of the words. This practice is not only discriminatory in terms of instructional objectives, but occasions feelings of inferiority for a possibly large segment of the class.)

When conventionally structured materials are adapted for use under a self-pacing system, such as PMI/MS— when the rate of materials consumption comes under the control of mastery criteria—conventional materials tend to be consumed at a very rapid rate. For example, the MIND learning materials to which 100 hours of instruction had been devoted in the control group situation at New York Telephone were consumed in less than half that time for the majority of the students who had experienced the PMI/MS version of MIND. Actually, this is in no way surprising, for in the conventional "lock-step" classroom, students' natural motivation to learn is given no outlet.

The implications of this accelerated materials consumption feature of all "continuous progress" or "individually tracked" learning systems for curriculum planning are numerous and weighty indeed, and well deserve discussion, quite probably of book length. The point I feel it is important to note here concerns the short term, in particular, the situation in which an experimental application of PMI/MS is being contemplated in a school setting where such has never been tried before. Specifically, it should be anticipated that whatever amount of instructional time had heretofore been devoted to a particular syllabus via a particular set of instructional materials, under PMI/MS that length of time will be reduced, most probably substantially. In an industrial training environment, where time means money, this is unquestionably a virtue inasmuch at it would permit a shortening of the training period. But in the public school, where attendance requirements and learning proficiency as yet have nothing to do with one another, the curriculum planning specialist is compelled to give thought to what students will do when they have finished the sequence of activities. In the New York Telephone project, this issue was resolved, at least for the purposes of the experimental run, by incorporating a very time-consuming spelling activity into the MIND syllabus, thus, artificially and, from the point of view of the course's objectives, irrelevantly, extending the average length of time that it would take a student to complete the course. A second factor concerning the high rate of materials consumption, one of economic rather than logistic importance, was alluded to earlier on page 111 in the discussion of Learning Centers for the Jackson Project. In a self-pacing system students must be able to gain access to a wide range of materials, a range that far exceeds that of any textbook devoted to a specific grade. The most economical approach is to make texts available on a library basis. In this view, a Learning Center functions as a lending library.

The fine details of PMI/MS materials design are very important. Critical deficiencies may be totally defeating.

Very often, apparently small deficiencies can render an instructional system unworkable. For example, it was originally thought, for the Comprehension sub-system in the Jackson Project, that the "checker" would himself, after assessing the Student's work, wash off the scoring form. The review in Figure 32 still contains this procedure. It was very quickly observed, however, that this washing process was taking an inordinate amount of the checker's time. Queues were building to intolerable lengths. We promptly changed the system to have Students wash their own scoring forms.

Various guidelines exist and can be employed if the circumstances allow. To consider one fairly long example, the basic building block of peer-mediated instruction is the interactive learning task, a stereotyped synthetic activity with arbitrary rules and conventions. Its primary principle of design is to create a situation demanding of the student intensive exercise of particular behaviors that are components of the objectives of the course of study. For a learner to perform a learning task effectively, he must be able to perceive how the learning task works and he must be capable of performing the actions demanded of him. It is thus natural to evaluate the mediational (communications) aspect of learning tasks in terms of *comprehensional adequacy* and *procedural simplicity and economy.*

One of the most common origins of student non-performance on tasks that they apparently should be capable of learning from is the failure of the immediate environment to communicate effectively to the learner what he is supposed to do, how he is supposed to do it, and then to check, through careful observation of what he in fact does, to make sure that he has understood all of this. In the classroom, the intrinsic nonexplicitness of natural language, coupled with the fact that too many teachers act as if they were responsible merely to *tell* students things, frequently leads to mediational failures. The student who fails under such circumstances does not fail for any cause that can be attributed to his competence, intelligence, or personality, however; he fails simply because he is confused.

Anomaly and *ambiguity* are the two principal villains. An anomalous situation arises when it is impossible for the student to figure out the intent of a message, hence when it is impossible for him to know what to do next, or to know what next to expect from the environment. Ambiguity exists when the message from the environment bears a multiplicity of interpretations, again a situation in which the learner cannot act with confidence.

A third aspect of comprehensional adequacy is *mediational redundancy.* It is usually wasteful of the learner's time to interfere persistently with his progress in a manner that he perceives as irrelevant to his successful performance of the task at hand. Too often, such extraneous communications result in the student's becoming frustrated (through boredom) and annoyed. Mediational redundancy can most frequently be observed in excessive repetition of instructions and excessive remediational information, which often results from over-diagnosing the student's errors in greater detail than is actually required for him to improve his performance.

All three of these factors, anomaly, ambiguity, and redundancy, should clearly be minimized when designing a learning task. By the same token, these criteria can provide useful measuring sticks in evaluating the mediational effectiveness of learning tasks.

Very often, a learning task will demand performance by the learner of skills that are not themselves representative of the skills to be learned, but are indirectly supportive of activities by which these skills can be addressed. For example, the Teacher procedures of PMI Spelling require pupils to become proficient in remediational and scoring procedures, neither of which is an instructional goal in itself, but both of which are of critical importance to the attainment of such skills. All too frequently, particularly in the early phases of a course, a student is inhibited or intimidated simply because he is not familiar with the procedures of a learning system. Since the supporting sub-skills required by a learning task are just that, *supporting,* not in themselves constituting course objectives, no purpose is served by constructing tasks in which the primary challenge is to acquire these skills. The primary challenge in any learning task should involve a goal skill uniquely. And so, ideally, the complexity of sub-skills that are merely supportive of the learning task should be reduced to a minimum.

The most useful measure of economy regarding the learning task is perhaps the ratio of the time spent with

Figure 40. A single-cue exercise item.

**Rhymes with**   **Fish**

Figure 41. A double-cue exercise item.

a goal skill to the time spent with supporting skills. For example, it is common in early grade spelling textbooks to use picture exercises to conjure a phonetic entity in the mind of the learner, which he is then to spell (see Figure 40). Clearly, this learning task involves not just a goal skill, but also a supporting skill, namely, the skill that is involved in figuring out what word is in fact to be spelled. The learner must first come up with that word; then he must spell it. Ideally, the word discovery process should be instantaneous, since the skill involved is merely supportive. Learning time should be spent spelling words, not figuring out what words are to be spelled.

What happens in practice for such exercises is that the little pictures are frequently anomalous or ambiguous, with the result either that the incorrect word is conjured or that the student is forced to ask a question or simply that it takes him longer to figure out what word is being specified. Thus such exercises do not present a particularly favorable ratio of goal skill time to supporting skill time. Notice, however, that this exercise could be greatly improved in a very simple manner just by supplying the learner, in addition to the little picture, a rhyming word (Figure 41). Now the learner is exposed to _two_ cues in two different modalities, with the probability greatly increased that he will correctly identify the word to be spelled and that he will perform this process more rapidly than he would have with the single cue. Thus, the second learning task is superior to the first from the point of view of the ratio of goal skill time to supporting skill time.

Neither PMI, nor any other instructional control system, will survive a deficient incentive system.

For the typical student in the schools, subject matter learning is rarely a central concern; even less frequently is it seen as an end in itself. More important to the student is the exploration of opportunities for action in the learning environment and the consequences associated with these opportunities; the technology, in other words, of personal survival and personal success. The student's perception of how the consequences of various actions are structured has therefore a great deal to do with whether the learning system will achieve its stated aims.

A classroom incentive system, which includes the incentives that actually do exist in the learning environment *and* the schedule according to which incentives are converted into realities, is important because it hinges on self-interest. Generally people decide on actions in terms of possible outcomes (and, most commonly, according to how these outcomes relate to self-interest: "Which is better for me?). These possible outcomes *are* the incentive system. If subject matter learning is a by-product of the classroom living experience, the contents and logic of the incentive system itself are the direct educational product of this experience. Subject matter learning may be a professed purpose of the schools, but this purpose will be achieved only to the extent that students are induced to act toward that purpose.

During the period of IBM research activities in computer-assisted instruction reported earlier, many visitors representing diverse educational interests would attend CAI demonstrations at the Thomas J. Watson Research Center. Frequently, visitors would show special interest in IBM's foreign language drills, which included such exercises as translation, dictation, substitution-transformation, and oral comprehension. One unique feature of these drills (which the visitor performed as would a student, via an audio-visual typewriter terminal) was that the student could see the correct answer any time he wanted simply by striking a certain key combination on the keyboard. A surprisingly large number of visitors, the majority *not* being classroom teachers, would protest that "This feature can't work. You know how kids are; they're out to beat the system. They'll surely abuse the correct answer option." But this is exactly the point. Of course, kids are out to beat the system, along with plenty of adult company. The challenge is to design a learning environment in which two conditions will hold: first, the student will at all times feel that he is optimizing his own actions, is pursuing his most advantageous course of action, is beating the system as best he can *as he sees it;* second, every action that the student in fact undertakes is an action appropriate to the instructional procedure, in other words, is exactly what the instructional system designer intends him to be doing.

A very important measure of adequacy for any learning environment is the degree to which the motivational values upon which the incentive system is built are actually in accord with the motivational values as held by students. An outcome to some action is not an incentive functionally unless the actor sees it as an incentive. A common problem in urban schools is the very limited understanding that seems to be possessed by curricular and instructional personnel of the kinds of things that students of varying backgrounds (cultures) see as incentives at various ages. In our worst schools, incentives that might encourage exploratory responses from the learner barely exist. In schools where mere restraint of action is the primary principle of order, negative sanctions replace incentives with the result that students acquire a defensive outlook toward living rather than an outlook fostering creative responses to novel experiences. It would be futile to implement a PMI system in a learning environment where sanctions take the place of incentives; for PMI systems demand the voluntary cooperation of the student.

PMI/MS has a wide range of subject matter applicability, but is not a panacea.

The research reported in this book deals exclusively, although certainly not comprehensively, with what are generally referred to as language skills. This fact has less to do with inherent limitations of PMI systems than with the exigencies of the cooperative field research endeavors in which I had an opportunity to engage. The PMI concept is nominally applicable to skills in general. That is, favorable outcomes could equally well be expected from an implementation in elementary school arithmetic as in elementary school spelling. However, any reader with classroom teaching experience will be aware that Peer-Mediated Instruction is not a *total* learning system either by nature or by design (although it can, as in the New York Telephone experience, approach totality in particular subject matters). There is little doubt that the PMI concept can be extended much more broadly than the intentional near-sightedness of this presentation would suggest. Still, there will be many instructional settings in which PMI mechanics are simply inappropriate, as on occasions when learners must, by virtue of circumstance, study in isolation from other learners. There will be situations in which an entirely different form of peer teaching might be called for, as for example in the case of complex industrial skills, where it is the journeyman-apprentice relationship that must be simulated. There will be aspects of the manifest and latent curriculum that cannot be operationally defined with great specificity and, hence, will not permit a straightforward PMI rendering. Even in those subject matters for which a PMI treatment might seem particularly appropriate, practical limitations may exist. For example, in the foreign language instruction context, it is at least problematic whether in interactive learning activities one student can efficiently remediate the pronunciational fluency of his peer, for here, assessment of performance is an exceedingly sophisticated enterprise. On the other hand, the foreign language sub-skills of reading, writing, and listening appear to be readily adaptable to the PMI modality. Finally, there will be situations in which a PMI application may be well conceived in all pedagogical respects, but will fail to produce anticipated results because of unfortunately inhospitable circumstances regarding the larger classroom, school, and social contexts. PMI is totally dependent upon at least a neutral, or in any event non-destructive, attitude on the part of students. In short, PMI possesses substantial intrinsic extensibility, but it is no panacea.

Two points are important: First, PMI should not be viewed as a *total* instructional system, an all-or-nothing proposition. Its use should be contemplated only for that particular inventory of skills whose acquisition would truly be facilitated by peer mediation. If PMI enhances aspects of reading, writing, and listening in foreign language work, but not speaking, then we should conceive our system, its syllabus and operations schedule, so as to include only the former. But the second point is of equal importance. Notwithstanding the research reported herein, very little is understood at the present time about the theoretical potential of PMI, in particular about what skills can and cannot be addressed through PMI *in principle;* this is to say that the only limits on applicability known to exist at the present time are the limits of human inventiveness and imagination. It may be that I personally have not been able to invent an interactive activity dealing with diction or pronunciation, but that in no way implies that the next designer won't come up with a beautiful scheme.

And so, the instructional engineer should start with the belief that PMI is generally applicable to skills. He should further accept that PMI formats and procedures may in principle and will in practice differ not only as subject matters differ, but also as ages and, possibly, socioeconomic identifications differ. What is important to keep in mind, however, is that the form of a particular version of a PMI system becomes a criterion of adequacy only in relation to the learning goals for which that system was conceived in the first place. Form is both a guide and an artifact in the fulfillment of a purpose. Putting together a particular version of PMI will inevitably require some new solutions to problems that have previously (for example, as described in this book) been solved in different ways.

PMI is favorably received and works well with students of many ages (from first grade through adulthood) and socioeconomic identifications. It is especially effective for students of average or below average ability.

This is true probably for many reasons. For one thing, the interactional intensity of learning through peer mediation is unequalled by the traditional teacher-focused mode of instructional communication. It is important to take note here of how modern electronic media technology has created in most of our society a positive thirst for media stimulation. What unimaginable boredom must accompany sitting quietly, doing little or nothing, in a classroom. PMI is a medium that demands response, demands interaction; like television, it is a cool medium. It involves the communicant; it induces action. Inevitably, the student prefers it to his previous and, perhaps, still present (in other subject matter areas), experiences with being taught. He can now actively participate in his own learning. Socioeconomic identification does not change this general picture, probably because *all* students experience the above cited effects of conventional instruction in some significant degree.

A second factor in accounting for the cooperation that PMI seems to foster might simply be that students, in the same degree as "real people," find satisfaction in working together. This impulse, after all, is what accounts for civilization. It would not be surprising, therefore, that students would respond well to a civilizing, as opposed to a fragmenting, mechanism. Perhaps, too, it is a useful and important side-effect of PMI that it fosters and supports this positive social value.

Thirdly, students no doubt like PMI because it is something new, and as such has some intrinsic interest. But this newness wears off after the first few weeks of instruction, so it is questionable how large a factor in the total is the mere fact of novelty.

Students start to take responsibility for their own learning.

Soon after students master the mechanics of PMI, they themselves become the guardians of the system. That is to say, students take over and run it. The problem with conventional instruction is that the student is given no responsibility. So how can he be expected to learn to act responsibly? A PMI learning system operates on a different premise: that students will respond favorably to systems for whose maintenance they are directly responsible. Not only does such a responsibility seem not to be regarded as a chore by students, but they often tend to guard the system zealously, continuing to make sure that every student who has a critical job in the system is performing that job. PMI is a communal and largely self-regulating social order, one that is well received to an extent that apparently compels responsible behavior on behalf of its maintenance.

Peer-Mediated Instruction is a peer-mediated social system

It is of great consequence to bear in mind that Peer-Mediated Instruction is first and foremost a social system in which the execution of specific rule-governed patterns of behavior merely happen to result in what we think of as instruction. This fact is particularly relevant to the issue of establishing priorities for further research involving the PMI methodology. One of the reasons that the PMI systems reported on earlier may work as well as they appear to is that, although a synthetic social system, PMI is apparently compatible with the broader social system that conditions the perspective of the student, his "real" world. Quite likely, PMI accords with what many students tacitly understand to be an important technique of real world survival, mainly, peer learning in general. Thus, the ultimate goal should be not only to explore other possible applications of the Peer-Mediated Instruction concept as developed in this book, but also, and perhaps ultimately more importantly, to explore in detail how social systems that pre-exist in the classroom may be harnessed in such a manner as to facilitate learning. This is precisely the approach to be taken by anthropologist Francis A.J. Ianni in a Ford Foundation study being conducted at Teachers College. Ianni states the problem in the project proposal this way:

Despite the increasing evidence that more socialization and probably more learning takes place in peer-mediated social systems in the high school, we know little about the optimum organization to facilitate such learning and nothing about how such systems intersect with the formal organization of the school.

If experience with the PMI serves as any indication of what may be expected from furthering our understanding of the relationship between social systems and learning systems, I can think of few lines of inquiry that hold greater promise.

PMI in relation to tutorial instruction.

I have said nothing as yet about the relation between PMI and other implementations of the "peer teaching" concept. It has not been my intention to imply through omission that in this instructional genre PMI is either the only, the first, or the best. So, for the record, let me state that the large number of good experiments carried out to test quite different engineering concepts of the peer instruction idea (in its general form) reveal an astonishingly high level of success vis-à-vis both significance *and* magnitude. As Jerome Bruner reflects in his review of *Children Teach Children,**

It has long been obvious that children learn from their peers, but a more significant observation is that *children learn from teaching other children.* From this a major educational strategy follows: namely, that every child must be given the opportunity to play the teaching role, because it is through playing this role that he may really learn how to learn.

Mobilization for Youth, a New York City antipoverty program, states that over a five-month period in which older children tutored younger children with reading difficulties, those tutored gained 6.0 months, while the tutors gained an extraordinary 3.4 years. *A leap of this magnitude is the order of achievement that must be striven for in the schools of America.*

The experience of the 1960s seems to indicate that the key to learning is individualization, and the use of the student or pupil as a teacher is one way to increase this individualization.

---

* Review of Alan Gartner, Mary Kohler, and Frank Reissman, *Children Teach Children* (New York: Harper & Row, 1971), in *Saturday Review,* January 15, 1972.

The concept of learning through teaching appears to be one of those basic ideas which do work, and it is finding a place in an enormous variety of settings . . . where the entire school is directed toward becoming a "tutorial community."

The work reported in *Peer-Mediated Instruction* merely adds to the list, although from what I can discern, PMI may be one of the small set that promises broad and practical *near-term* application.

The Last Word.

To the best of my knowledge, I coined the term "peer-mediated instruction" (in contrast to "teacher-mediated instruction") and the abbreviation PMI. Originally, it had been my intention to preserve the term and its abbreviation for its reference to the mechanics of a specific interactive process; that is, to *immediate selective correction* and *differential assignment of work.* As the terms have come into circulation at Teachers College, they have taken on a new life. For, as students and colleagues are continually suggesting to me (occasionally flogging me with), there are numerous interesting and potentially useful configurations of the peer teaching process. And "peer-mediated instruction" is a congenial cover term for all of these. So be it. Word meanings still remain largely beyond the domain of effective control of the average individual.

But this book is the odyssey of a specific idea traveling along a specific route of growth and development. No matter what fate may befall the term in its own odyssey, here is how PMI began.

PMI/MS Manual

Department of
Environmental Research and Development

Urban Education Projects

INSTRUCTIONAL MANAGEMENT SYSTEM — APPLIED TO REMEDIAL READING

Peter Rosenbaum with Jerry Barney
Teachers College, Columbia University

HORACE MANN-LINCOLN INSTITUTE

Teachers College

Columbia University in the City of New York

THE PEER-MEDIATED INSTRUCTIONAL MANAGEMENT SYSTEM (PMI/MS):

An Application in Remedial Reading and Basic Language Skills*

Designed by Peter Rosenbaum

with the assistance of Jerry Barney

*The design process for the application of PMI/MS herein de-
scribed was funded in part by a grant from the American
Telephone and Telegraph Company. This document has not been
approved for public release or sale; its distribution is limited.

Applications Manual

RR-0006-LR

July 1971

PREFACE

Reading ability is needed even for jobs that require the simplest skills
in our business. Yet this is an ability most lacking in many new job appli-
cants. Several System companies now find it necessary to provide remedial
reading assistance before many new employees can be trained for entry level
jobs. A review of the reading programs being used by the companies revealed
that results vary widely.

The Urban Education section of the Department of Environmental Affairs
working in conjunction with Teachers College, Columbia University, developed
an Instructional Management System for remedial adult courses in English reading. This manual is a prototype of this Instructional Management System that
will accommodate practically all commercially available reading materials and
provides for continued individual assessment of the person receiving training.

Application and refinement of this system was conducted at the East
Harlem Center of Columbia Teachers College. Further testing of this prototype
was conducted in the New York Telephone Company Training Center.

The Instructional Management System described in this manual presents a
unique way of conducting courses in remedial reading for adults. The manual
is designed to be used by curriculum planning and training specialists.

PMI/MS (PEER-MEDIATED INSTRUCTIONAL MANAGEMENT SYSTEM), as the system is
referred to, is based on the "buddy" concept. Students spend almost all of
their time in class working in pairs, acting alternately as "Teacher" and
"Student." When acting as "Teacher," the trainee refers to a book containing

i

lesson plans for his "Student." Included in this book is all the information
the "Teacher" needs to make assignments, to score his "Student" responses,
and to assign appropriate new or review material based on his "Student's"
mastery of the required content. The "Student" proceeds through the required
material at his own pace while receiving immediate feedback as to the correctness of his performance and his progress from his "Teacher."

When a class is run this way, trainees can progress as rapidly as they
are able and spend extra time on those points most difficult for them. They
are not required to wait for the rest of the class before they can proceed,
nor are they permitted to leave a topic they are not sure of merely because
the majority of their classmates have already moved on.

This system, then, insures individualized instruction; it is the trainee's
own performance, and only his performance, that regulates his progress with a
given training material. Also, because each trainee must grasp each part of the
course before he is allowed to move on, there is no uncertainty about what an
individual trainee is supposed to learn.

Finally, there is no uncertainty in the mind of the trainee as to the
correctness of his performance; he is told immediately whether his response
is right or wrong, and if he makes a mistake, he is immediately provided with
remediational information.

PMI/MS, then, uses the buddy system to implement a course of instruction
based on a preselected sequencing of content which insures individualized yet
uniform teaching. Because PMI/MS is a <u>system</u> for implementing a course rather
than a course syllabus, it contains no content material. It is up to a curriculum planner or trainer to choose an appropriate syllabus and "plug it into" the

ii

system by specifying the order in which content is presented, the degree of mastery required, etc. A syllabus may be chosen from among the wide range of commercially produced remedial reading programs or may be the creation of the curriculum planner.

Using this system can greatly reduce the time required to teach remedial reading and do it more effectively than at present. The classroom instructor is also free to give individual assistance to those trainees with special problems.

This approach to the learning of factual material needs more tests with a variety of materials but has a great potential for any educational program that has intellectual knowledge and skill objectives.

Department of Environmental Affairs
American Telephone and Telegraph Company
July, 1971

Table of Contents
Page

Preface
i

Designer's Note
1

1.0 PMI/MS: Basic Concepts
7

2.0 PMI/MS: Details of Implementation
10

2.1 Content Considerations
10

2.2 How Students Spend Their Time
11

2.3 How the Student Perceives the Sequence of Activities
19

2.4 How the Curriculum Planner Perceives the Sequence of Activities
22

2.5 What the Teacher (the trainee, not his classroom instructor) Does
25

2.6 How the Scoring System Works
29

3.0 PMI/MS: Review of Materials and Personnel Functions
33

3.1 Materials
33

3.2 Personnel Functions
35

4.0 PMI/MS: Details of Administration
35

4.1 Facilities
35

4.2 Procedures for Pairing Trainees
36

4.3 Teacher Down-time
41

4.4 What the PMI/MS Instructor Does
42

4.5 What the PMI/MS Administrator Does
46

4.6 Criterion Testing
48

4.7	Start-up Guidelines	48
4.8	PMI/MS Operations Chronology	50
4.9	Charts and Graphs of Use in Monitoring PMI/MS Operations	51
5.0	PMI/MS: Designing Your Own	50
5.1	Starting Out	53
5.2	The Necessary Materials	55
5.3	The Use of Sequence Numbers	55
5.4	Updating the Syllabus	55

A Sample from a Text (MIND)	Appendix A
Paper Forms Used by PMI/MS	Appendix B
A Sample Student Activity Checklist	Appendix C
A Sample Teacher Activity Checklist	Appendix D
MIND Correct Answer Forms	Appendix E

Designer's Note

The buddy system is a teaching concept that generally evokes
pleasant associations for practicing teachers and for former students
alike. Those with experience as classroom instructors candidly state
that students enjoy working with each other; that they work, on average,
much more productively when they can work together; and that this social
experience is a valuable educational experience besides.

Buddy systems are what PMI/MS is all about -- a simple way to use
existing materials of instruction, e.g., textbook practice workbooks, in
a buddy system classroom format.

PMI/MS did not originate as a buddy system concept; rather, the
system is a direct spiritual descendant of a set of CAI (Computer-Assisted
Instruction) strategies developed in the course of IBM's CAI research at
the Thomas J. Watson Research Center in Yorktown Heights, N.Y.

The fact that well-conceived CAI can and does lead to increases
in instructional output in skills subject matters or skills aspects of other
subject matters has been well publicized, as, for example, in the numerous
accounts of the work of Suppes at Stanford and Adams at IBM. What has received less publicity, however, is the fact that these learning gains are
attributable less to the hardware aspect of CAI than they are to the pedagogical wisdom built into the CAI software, the programs that control the
responses of the computer to the student. The programs developed by Adams,
for example, always gave students individually tailored remediation, pin-
pointing the student's errors for him, and often, suggesting an improvement;

1

Adams' program also insured that a student would get as much practice as he
needed to be able to satisfy the requirements of the lesson (<u>variable length
assignments</u>, in essence). In effect, the CAI student could carry on a continuous instructional dialogue with a highly accurate and proficiency-oriented
<u>supervisor</u>. That such applications of CAI have been successful
comes as a fact of no great surprise when one contrasts the pedagogical quality
of this kind of CAI experience with the experiences offered in the typical
classroom setting.

The quintessential notion underlying PMI/MS is that the critical supervisory functions that are attended to by a machine in CAI can, in principle,
be attended to by a trainee in a special version of the buddy system, one in
which trainees play alternating Teacher and Student roles. Not only, could
it be reasoned, might the trainee functioning as a Student derive all the
benefits of the CAI trainee, but so might the trainee functioning as a Teacher
derive special benefits accruing from his special role in relation to his
buddy.

In a spirit of hopefulness, a program of design and development was
undertaken in September of 1969 by the Horace Mann-Lincoln Institute at
Teachers College, Columbia University, the end product of which was to be the
software package to support what is now being called Peer-Mediated Instruction
Management System (PMI/MS). As is suggested by the slash, PMI/MS was developed
in two phases, the first to develop peer-mediation techniques and test them out;
and the second to develop and test a system of practical classroom management
for peer-mediated instruction, which would link peer-mediation to the content
and materials available for use in a course.

2

Four projects summarize the field studies to date of PMI/MS. By subject matter, these are as follows:

Spelling. An application of PMI/MS to the exclusive subject matter of spelling was given a field trial during the 1970 summer session for two classes of 3rd graders at P.S. 129 in Manhattan. This project confirmed the essential soundness of several basic peer-mediation techniques. Also, it showed that peer-mediation is both possible and desirable in the classroom from the instructor's point of view. The method showed considerable promise of being adopted as a new approach to spelling.

ESL. Daniel Parrish, a graduate student at Teachers College, has recently concluded research in which he designed and tested an application of PMI/MS for adult education in the subject matter of English as a second language. This program was implemented at a service school of the Manpower & Career Development Agency on Staten Island in New York City. This research strongly suggests that the peer-mediation methodology is readily adaptable to subject matter very different from 3rd grade spelling. Further, it proved itself adaptable to students of greatly different age and background from the populations on which it was previously tested.

Reading -- Phase One. In both of the foregoing experimental applications, content was specially authored for the purpose. The reading project undertaken at the Teachers College-supported Community Resources Center at 117th Street and 3rd Avenue in Manhattan was the first operational test of the management system component of PMI/MS in which peer-mediation was to be applied to an arbitrary set of instructional materials. The student population for the project was drawn primarily from Brandeis High School in Manhattan. This project although not intended as a full scale effectiveness test for PMI/MS, was informative on a number of important points: First, that the creation of PMI/MS software materials can be a fairly straightforward process, one that can profit from imagination, but one that can, with good results, be carried out in a mechanical way; second, that the dynamics of the communication that goes on between two buddies under PMI/MS can be learned and used even by students with severe deficits in reading ability.

Reading -- Phase Two. With noteworthy results, the version of PMI described in this manual was put into use during the first quarter of 1971 on an experimental basis with a class in a remedial reading training environment operated by the New York Telephone Company. Reports from this project appear to suggest that this new methodology is roughly twice as effective and four times as efficient as the conventional methodology with which it was compared.

This version of PMI/MS achieves its apparent superior performance as the result of two design features. First, the system tracks trainees individually and, thus, can in principle achieve economies of time that are not possible for lock-step methodologies. Second, and perhaps more to the point, PMI/MS trainees pace each other via a form of buddy system that has them performing in interactive, highly structured "Teacher" - "Student" roles, on an alternating basis. As a "Teacher", in which capacity a trainee serves for half of his total instructional time, the trainee 1) provides his peer with immediate remediation and correction of errors, and 2) executes a paper-and-pencil prescription procedure enabling him to assign differential amounts of work to his partner on the basis of the partner's demonstrated needs. A trainee advances through the syllabus only as (i.e., as fast as) he becomes capable of demonstrating pre-requisite levels of proficiency.

4

The most impressive statistic thus far to emerge from the New York Telephone project is an efficiency statistic that contrasts the PMI/MS methodology with the methodology previously employed in terms of the number of hours of instruction per student required to raise that student one measured grade level in reading vocabulary. The trial showed that PMI/MS cut in half the time required to teach New York Telephone's course in remedial reading and doubled the amount of reading improvement achieved by traditional classroom methods.

PMI/MS as described in this manual is not a set of instructional materials; it is a software system packaged in kit form for using existing materials in a new way. (The language skills materials produced by MIND, Inc. were used in the New York Telephone study.)

      *   *   *   *   *   *

This document is designed to be used by curriculum planning specialists in remedial language skills training environments as a guide to implementing PMI/MS. For these purposes, the responsible curriculum planning specialist could be any person on the instructional or curricular staff who has had some classroom experience and is familiar with the special characteristics of the trainee population and the subject matter.

Whether a PMI/MS learning environment will be successful in a particular instance depends very largely on the attention that has been given to detail during the implementation. While no formal preparation in instructional

5

system is needed to apply PMI/MS to remedial reading and related language skills, it is important for the responsible curriculum planner to become thoroughly familiar with the approach presented in the body of this manual.

The reader should be aware of how the manual handles the special semantic problems which arise from the role-playing that goes on under PMI/MS. The following glossary is essential to comprehension:

"Student" means "trainee acting in a special role."

"Teacher" means "trainee acting in a second special role."

"Classroom Instructor" means "the supervising teacher"

Peter Rosenbaum

Teachers College

July 1971

1.0   PMI/MS: Basic Concepts

The most natural place to begin the exposition is with a view of what a PMI/MS classroom looks like when it is in operation.

1)   The visitor to such a classroom would be struck first by the intensity with which the trainees are involved in what they are doing. The room seems almost to hum, for there is so much low-level talking going on. Most trainees do not bother to look up when the visitor enters the room.

2)   The observer might not spot the classroom instructor immediately; but he would certainly observe that the trainees, if not working independently, are paired with one another, one providing some kind of practice and supervision for the other in a Teacher-Student relationship.

3)   Closer examination of this pair of peers would reveal that "Teachers" correct "Students'" work, providing immediate tailored remediation for them whenever necessary.

4)   It would also be seen that the length of time a Student spends on an activity is variable, and is directly related to how well he is performing that activity.

5)   Finally, the visitor would observe that the peer Teacher uses his Scoring Form as a mini-computer, to determine which of several alternative assignments should next be prescribed for the Student.

7

PMI/MS is a <u>peer-mediated</u> learning system, by which two things are meant:

1) Trainees exercise <u>full responsibility</u> for their own instructional progress.

2) Trainees provide <u>pacing</u> and <u>coaching</u> assistance, each for the other.

PMI/MS was conceived as a practical response to two well-known instructional problems. The first concerns the limited quantity of supervised practice that particular trainees can actually receive in conventionally structured <u>teacher-mediated</u> learning environments.

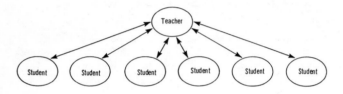

Fig. 1 — Communications Structure of a Teacher-Mediated Learning Environment.

Figure 1, as a model of the typical classroom, reveals that the amount of personal attention to be gotten by any one trainee will be directly related to the number of trainees in the class; hence, a problem arises. Even in small classes (10 to 14 trainees), no single trainee gets a

8

great deal of the instructor's personal attention, (although, of course, all of the instructor's time might be going for just that purpose). In larger classes, such as those not unusual in public school settings, personal supervision is nonexistent, (perhaps partially explaining why class size is so often found to be related to achievement).

PMI/MS offers a new and improved solution to the problem of inadequate personal supervision.

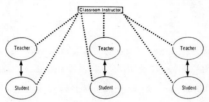

Fig. 2 – Communications structure of a peer-mediated learning environment. Labels "Teacher" and "Student" refer to students taking roles.

PMI/MS requires each trainee to divide his time equally between being a Teacher and a Student, thus assuring equal instructional advantage to all trainees. Each trainee in PMI/MS classroom is guaranteed personal supervision for no less than half of the total instructional time to be spent under PMI/MS. And, of course, while he is not acting as a Student, the PMI/MS trainee is performing as a Teacher for one of his peers, apparently learning a very great deal through these experiences. Note well that both experiences, Student and Teacher, are learning experiences. Also, the instructional benefits of PMI/MS are independent of class size.

The other side of the coin from the lack of opportunity to perform (hence, practice) is lack of involvement; even in the best-intentioned teacher-mediated classrooms, a sustained level of involvement for any

9

particular student is an impossibility. Non-involvement, to whatever
extent it exists, inevitably induces the student to turn off or tune
out.

PMI/MS fosters a great deal of continuous interpersonal communication based upon the role requirements of Teacher and Student. The
use of the system results in a noticeably increased degree of legitimate
involvement on the part of the trainee.

Possible Question:

1)   Does PMI/MS run all of the time in a classroom? It can, but
it doesn't need to. PMI/MS is a sub-system that runs under the control
of the classroom instructor, who brings the system up at his (or her)
discretion.

2.0   PMI/MS: Details of Implementation

2.1   Content Considerations

2.1.1   PMI/MS is not a set of instructional materials or tests: it
is not competitive with textbooks or instructional media; it is a
management system for using existing instructional materials and texts.
PMI/MS bears the same relation to particular materials of instruction
that a computer operating system bears to particular programming
languages (e.g., FORTRAN) and content. A curriculum designer programs
materials of instruction for use under PMI/MS. (As with a computer
program, excellence of design is an ideal attained with a widely varying
degree of success.)

The first operational test of PMI/MS, upon which this manual is based, involved the use of the widely used language skills materials developed by MIND, Inc.* This large textbook, along with its associated tapes, was the basis of "English" instruction in the New York Telephone Company test environment. However, though the following descriptive discussion will be couched in terms of these MIND materials, all commercially available instructional materials for remedial reading and remedial basic language skills, as far as we are aware, can be adapted for PMI/MS use at marginal cost in time and effort.

2.2   How Students Spend Their Time

The detail that determines a trainee's activities under PMI/MS at any given moment, is whether he is performing as Student, or as Teacher. At all times, the PMI/MS trainee is functioning as one or the other.

A Student (i.e., the trainee role-playing as Student) engages in two kinds of learning activities, independent study activities and supervised activities. The exact mix of these two depends primarily upon the texts being used, more exactly upon the kinds of learning activities employed in the texts and their distribution in lessons. The distribution outline in the following sections is unique to the MIND materials. (However, many other equally promising content configurations for MIND are conceivable.)

---

*MIND: Language Skills Development, MIND, Inc. (Stamford, Conn. 1967).

2.2.1   The MIND text suggests three kinds of <u>independent</u> study activities.

<u>Vocabulary, Syntax, and Morphology Study</u>. Systematically distributed
throughout the MIND textbook are brief presentational units in which
linguistic information in various categories is communicated to the
Student. (The MIND excerpt in Appendix A demonstrates vocabulary and
morphology units, e.g., pp. A1-A10.)

<u>Reading</u>. In each MIND "skill group" there exists a passage that
the Student is to read (as, for example, in Appendix A, pp. A10-A12).

<u>Critical Review</u>. The critical review is not a MIND assignment
at all.

For improvement in reading comprehension, the MIND text relies rather
heavily on the group discussion of a passage read by all trainees at the
same time (e.g., A10-A13). However, individual differences (and, hence,
learning rate) promises to be such under PMI/MS that having the trainees
arrive at the same reading assignment on the same day was out of the
question. Thus, the group discussion technique could not be used. Some
other approach to reading for comprehension had to be created, to wit,
the <u>critical review</u>.

During the PMI/MS orientation period for trainees, classroom instructors
would explain that improvement of the school experience and, in particular,
the content of the overall instructional program is the responsibility
not only of the training staff, but of the trainees as well. One way
in which trainees can help, is by evaluating the quality and personal

12

relevance of the reading assignments contained in the program that
they, as Students, are asked to perform. The <u>critical review</u> activity
asks a Student to evaluate reading he has just done. A special Reader's
Evaluation Form (See Fig. 3) is provided for the purpose and is present
in the classroom. This form permits the Student to vote on whether the
passage should be continued or discontinued for the next class cycle.
It also requests an account of his reasoning--why the Student voted the
way he did. It is very important that the trainees give reasons. For
if they merely vote, then the curriculum specialist will have no constraining information on what to replace excluded literature with.

   The critical review could likely be a mainstay of any PMI/MS implementation for remedial reading, regardless of text materials, and particularly
if these materials are lacking in reading comprehension exercises. For
one thing, the opportunity to participate in the course design process
can be a powerful inducement to attentive reading for many trainees,
the kind of reading that probably leads most directly to reading improvement. Secondly, the critical review gives the trainee an opportunity
to communicate in writing <u>with perceived purpose</u>, an educational experience of known importance and one that can be particularly difficult to
achieve. And thirdly, the Reader's Evaluation Forms produced by the
trainees during the operation of PMI/MS will indeed enable the curriculum
staff to improve the quality of the reading materials offered to Students
in subsequent versions of the program.

   There is little doubt that the Student could be asked to evaluate
reading passages according to other criteria than those printed on the

READER'S EVALUATION FORM

NAME _____   SEQUENCE NO: _____

DATE _____

This reading should be:

kept in the program ☐   ☐ not kept in the program

Reasons:

_____
_____
_____
_____
_____
_____
_____
_____
_____
_____
_____
_____
_____
_____
_____
_____
_____
_____
_____

Fig. 3 – The Reader's Evaluation Form- - NYT Version

14

Reader Evaluation Form in Figure 6. For example, alternate versions of
the form can readily be prepared that might query the Student on the
relevance of the passage to his life, or on the qualities of the passage
that make it interesting. The one caution that must be observed, however,
in redesigning the evaluation form concerns the possibility of increasing
the demand made upon the trainer's time. For example, it is generally
acknowledged by English teachers that the writing of a synopsis can be
a useful comprehension exercise (as well as a writing exercise). However,
if such an exercise is to achieve its full potential as a learning
activity, it should be carefully criticized by the instructor and reviewed
by the instructor with the trainee to whatever extent the trainee's performance requires such review. Thus, a small change in the PMI materials
can result in a greatly increased demand on a trainer's time, a demand
which may not in practice be reasonable.

2.2.2   Supervised activities are those peer-mediated interactions in
which a Student works with a Teacher. The performance drills of the MIND
text are conceptually reducible to just three elementary exercise types.

   Selection exercises. The Student must select the correct item or
items from a set of visible or otherwise known possibilities. (See
Appendix A, p. A14, "C.")

   Transformation exercises. The Student must transform a given word
or sentence into a target word or sentence either by deleting things from
the original, replacing things in it, or by moving its elements around.
(See Appendix A, pp. A5-A6, "SECTION 6" and "SECTION 7.")

<u>Dictation exercises</u>. The Student listens to a message and must write
the correct written form of what he hears, as in a spelling drill based
on vocabulary words. (See Appendix A, pp. A9–A10.)

These exercises are all carried out through a structured dialogue
that goes on between a Student and his Teacher. The following flowchart shows how this dialogue is achieved. Here are some definitions
that will simplify the interpretation of the flowchart.

LARGE RECTANGLE A <u>process</u> executed either by the Teacher (marked
by the letter T in the upper left hand corner) or by the Student (marked
by the letter S).

LARGE DIAMOND A <u>decision</u> made either by a Teacher (T) or by a
Student (S) and leading to one of two alternative courses of action.

ARROW The <u>flow</u> of time.

Following this chart as it describes the interaction for a spelling
activity of the Dictation variety, one observes:

The Teacher dictates a word (which he himself reads from the text)
to be spelled by the Student.

The Student listens and writes what he believes to be the correct
spelling on his pad. He passes his pad to the Teacher.

The Teacher compares the Student's response with the correct answer
(which the Teacher finds in an answer-book version of the text; see
Section 3.1.6). If the response is incorrect, the Teacher provides corrective feedback by crossing out the misspelled portion of the word and

16

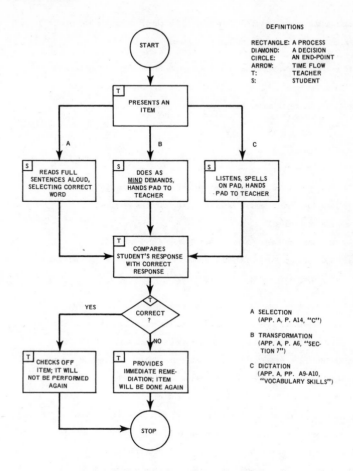

DEFINITIONS

RECTANGLE: A PROCESS
DIAMOND: A DECISION
CIRCLE: AN END-POINT
ARROW: TIME FLOW
T: TEACHER
S: STUDENT

A SELECTION
(APP. A, P. A14, "C")

B TRANSFORMATION
(APP. A, P. A6, "SEC-
TION 7")

C DICTATION
(APP. A, PP. A9-A10,
"VOCABULARY SKILLS")

Fig. 4 - Communications outcomes within a single exercise item for
supervised activities based upon MIND. (Since all written MIND exercises
had to be reconfigured as interactive verbal PMI/MS activities, the reader
will detect essential discrepancies of form between a MIND exercise and
its PMI/MS analogue, but never discrepancies of content.)

17

by spelling the word correctly (based upon the text) alongside the misspelled version. He then goes on to the next item.

If the Student's response is correct, the Teacher will flag this
item (via an appropriately placed check on his Scoring Form) so that the
word will not be represented later on. The Teacher then goes on to the
next item.

Possible Questions:

1) What is a Scoring Form? See Sections 2.5 and 2.6

2) How does a Teacher know what to do? See Section 2.5

3) How do correct answer materials fit into the picture?
See Section 3.1

4) How does a Teacher score? See Sections 2.5 and 2.6.

5) How closely do the PMI/MS exercise types have to be matched with
the text exercises? See Section 2.2.3.

2.2.3   Summarizing the life of a Student under PMI/MS, he engages
either in independent study activities or in supervised activities. The
matching of PMI/MS exercise types to text is a technical skill with an
important intuitive aspect. In this particular PMI/MS implementation
of the MIND syllabus, the stated activities suffice completely. Other
text materials might impose slightly different constraints on exercise
design; but for none of the materials that we have recently used or
reviewed have we found that PMI/MS implementation is either impossible
or in any way difficult to achieve. (We have intensively studied the
New Rochester Occupational Reading Series--SRA, the Programmed Training

Course, Directory Assistance and Intercept Operators--AT&T, and the <u>SRA</u>
<u>Reading Laboratory Kit, Level IIIb</u>--SRA.)

2.3   How the Student Perceives the Sequence of Activities

As a Student, the trainee sees the full extent of the tasks he is
being challenged with in the pages of his Student Activity Checklist, in
essence, a checklist for a sequence of ordered activities. (See Figure 5.)

Each <u>row</u> in the manual gives:

1)   the sequence number of the activity,

2)   an indication as to whether the activity is to be supervised
       (S) or independently performed (I),

3)   the location of the materials to be used,

4)   instructions for use (which may even be the instructions in
       the text itself),

5)   a checkoff-on-completion column.

The Student's task as he sees it, is to work his way through this checklist. (Appendix C is particularly worthwhile to examine, for it is a
section of the prototype Student Activity Checklist used in the New
York Telephone field study. Specifically, Appendix C contains a checklist for the "Skill Group C" section of the MIND materials contained in
Appendix A.)

The rules of the game, as seen by the Student, depend heavily on
whether the activity he is to do next is to be independently performed
or to be supervised.

When a Student completes an independent activity, he checks off
that activity on the checklist and goes on to the next activity in the

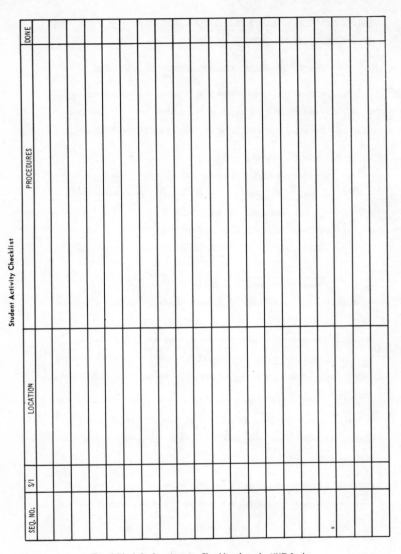

Fig. 5-Blank Student Activity Checklist from the NYT Study

checklist sequence.

When a Student completes a supervised activity, however, he is
informed <u>by his Teacher</u> which activities in the Student Activity Checklist
he is to turn to next. If the Student has demonstrated sufficient proficiency, he <u>may</u> find that his Teacher will advance him several Sequence
Numbers, exempting him (at least temporarily) from the assignments thus
passed over. It is also possible, depending on how the syllabus is
designed (see section 2.4), that the Teacher will reassign material
previously encountered by the Student. In this way, the Student can
be automatically paced by a criterion of mastery. (In the PMI/MS - MIND
syllabus created for the New York Telephone Company trial limited use
was made of these system features. See Section 2.47.)

It is very important to be aware that, from the Student's point of
view, he can reduce his load, often significantly. PMI/MS is not going
to require that he necessarily do every assignment. In fact, he knows
that he can be exempted from a great deal of work that others might have
to do. All that he must do is "convince" his Teacher that his performance
merits such exemption. (Section 2.5 starts the discussion of the mechanics
by which Teachers differentially allocate work.)

Possible Questions:
1) How does the Teacher differentially allocate work? See
    Sections 2.4 and 2.5.
2) The Teacher doesn't just make up arbitrary assignments, does
    he? No, all assignment options have been set up in advance by
    the PMI/MS curriculum planner. See Sections 2.4 and 2.5.
3) What does a Student Activity Checklist look like physically?
    See Section 3.1.
4) How is a Student Activity Checklist Made? See Sections 5.0-5.4.

21

2.4   How the Curriculum Planner Perceives the Sequence of Activities

PMI/MS is a system that uses published or otherwise pre-exisiting
materials of instruction. Virtually all such materials, as one would
expect, possess an implicit ordering of content and learning activities
which can be used as a sequencing base. The syllabus sequence in Figure
6 comes very close to being idential to sequence built into the basic
instructional unit of the MIND materials. The reader may find it in-
structive to contrast this sequence of PMI/MS activities with the MIND
text on which it is based. (See Appendix A.)

The Student Activity Checklist with the sequence number 350 instructs
the Student to study the linguistic content of the unit. Whenever the
Student feels he has mastered this material, he goes on to Seq. No. 360
which has him engage in supervised practice of the unit's content, advancement from which is entirely dependent upon the Student's attaining
a satisfactory level of proficiency as perceived by the Teacher. (Sections
2.5 and 2.6) Students requiring greater amounts of practice will find
that they are being asked to practice more, perhaps even through the
reassignment of material previously studied or performed.

Successfully graduating from the Word Attack Skills, the Student
is directed by his Teacher to Sequence Number 410, an independent study
activity involving MIND vocabulary. Then on to the reading passage;
and then the critical review of the reading passage (which is not, the
reader will recall, a MIND learning activity at all).

The Student then comes to a supervised activity in which the
challenge is to spell the vocabulary words (Spelling, like Reader's

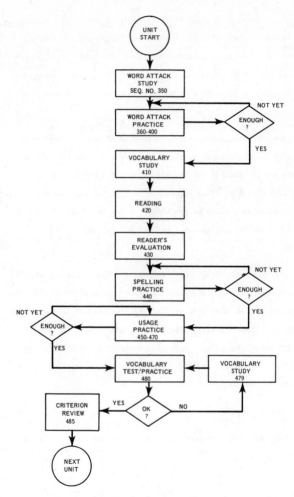

Fig. 6-The PMI/MS Sequence for "Skill Group C" In
Appendix A,pp. A2-A16.

23

Evaluation, supplements the activities prescribed in the MIND text.)
Upon satisfactory completion of the spelling assignment, the Student is
directed to a set of semantic and grammatical exercises based upon the
vocabulary, also under supervision. Upon completion, the Student is
finally directed on to a vocabulary practice activity, Sequence Number
480.

It is worth noting about this instructional sequence that only
one activity is supplemental to the obligatory sequence; that one is
the Vocabulary (Re)Study, Seq. No. 479, associated with the Vocabulary
Test/Practice activity. However, within each of the supervised activities
in the sequence, the amount of practice that any one Student is going
to do is very carefully regulated, as Sections 2.5 and 2.6 will inform
the reader.

The sequence of instructions described in Figure 6 is a fairly
direct adaptation of MIND materials. Keep in mind that PMI/MS syllabus
design allows a great deal more flexibility than the MIND design would
imply, for the Student Activity Checklist is blank initially and the
imagination and wisdom of the curriculum designer prevail. Thus, any
materials in the physical instructional environment (subject to logistic
considerations) can be freely used.

Possible Questions:

1) How does the flowchart in Figure 6 get made? By conceptualiza-
tion and construction. See Section 5.

24

2)   Which comes first in the development stage, the Student
      Activity Checklist or a syllabus like the one in Figure
      6? Some designers may be able to skip the syllabus stage
      and create the Student Activity Checklist directly,
      especially if a single text (e.g., MIND) or text series
      is involved. However, and especially in the light of
      the widespread availability of multi-media, a syllabus
      stage of development, or at least some lead time (e.g.,
      one full student cycle for the New York Telephone
      project) for thinking about the syllabus design, is
      probably essential.

2.5   <u>What the Teacher (the trainee, not his classroom instructor)
      Does</u>

There exists in the PMI/MS system, in addition to the Student
Activity Checklist, a form called a Teacher Activity Checklist. For
each Student Activity that calls for supervision, and only for those,
there exists a corresponding entry in the Teacher Activity Checklist.
This relationship can be observed by comparing Appendix D with Appendix
C, a Teacher Activity Checklist with its Student Activity Checklist.

As can be observed in Figure 7, a Teacher Activity Checklist is
specified by three fields of information. This form tells the Teacher
<u>what to do,</u> <u>how to score,</u> and <u>what activity to prescribe for the Student</u>
to do next. (The contents of these fields are specified by a curriculum
planner well in advance of their operational use in the classroom.)

25

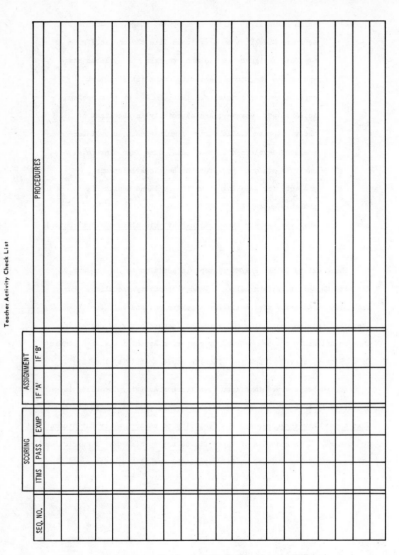

Fig. 7 – A blank page in a Teacher Activity Checklist from the NYT Study

2.5.1   The <u>Scoring</u> Field. This field contains three parameters, which are

    1)   the total number of items in the exercise, ITMS

    2)   the number of iterations ("loops," "passes") through the list of items that are allowed before the activity is to be terminated, PASS, and

    3)   the number of exemptions ("incorrect" or "untried" items) allowed to Students in this exercise, EXMP.

The supervised activity prescribed by the Seq. No. 480 in the Teacher Activity Checklist in Figure 8 contains 40 items with 4 exemptions allowed to the Student. Thus, the Student must get 36 out of 40 items correct (90% performance) and he is allowed 3 passes through the list to achieve this threshold performance level.

2.5.2   The <u>Assignment</u> Field. Here, finally, is the domain of options over which trainees (as Teachers) are permitted to make assignments for each other. The trainee functioning as Teacher administers a learning activity in accordance with the instructions in the Procedure Field. The Teacher monitors the performance of his Student by employing a scoring technique based upon a special Scoring Form. Depending on the outcome of the scoring process, the Teacher assigns one of two pre-existing (on the Teacher Activity Checklist) assignments in the Student Activity Checklist. (See SPECIAL NOTE Section 2.6)

2.5.3.   The <u>Procedure</u> Field. This field lists the procedures that the Teacher is to have the Student follow with respect to some specific activity. (In the MIND-based project at New York Telephone, instructions would fall into two classes. They were either specific instructions

Teacher Activity Check List

SEQ. NO.	SCORING			ASSIGNMENT		PROCEDURES
	ITMS	PASS	EXMP	IF 'A'	IF 'B'	
450	8	5	0	460	460	Standard procedures (copy scoring and assignment information onto a Scoring form; Student should follow Student Activity Checklist procedures; be sure Student does items in correct order, correct and score each item.
460	12	5	1	470	470	Standard procedures (see PROCEDURES on Seq. No. 450 above for more information on Standard procedures.)
470	10	5	1	480	480	Standard procedures (see #450).
480	40	3	4	485	479	Standard procedures.

Fig. 8 - page from a Teacher Activity Checklist from MIND (NYT Study, as in Appendix D).

intended to override the MIND instructions or the general rule "Follow
MIND instructions.")

Possible Questions:

1) How does the scoring system work? See Section 2.6.

2.6 How the Scoring System Works

When a Student requires the services of his Teacher, he has the
Teacher turn to the sequence number in the Teacher Activity Checklist
that corresponds to the sequence number that the Student is on in his
Student Book. The Teacher will then fill out a Scoring Form in the
manner by which the Scoring Form in Figure 9 is derived from Sequence
Number 480 in Figure 8.

1) The Teacher will record the header information, name of
    Student, date and sequence number.

2) Noting that the activity contains 40 items, the Teacher will
    darken box 41, thereby recording the number of different
    items to be performed.

3) The Teacher will then record the number of permissible passes
    (3) by darkening out box 4.

4) The Teacher, lastly, will fill in the "A" and "B" parameters
    indicating to which sequence number in his Student Manual
    the Teacher will send the Student to under different scoring
    circumstances.

SPECIAL NOTE: The Teacher is given no latitude in creating
prescriptions. He doesn't create them at all; he merely
assigns them. In filling out a scoring form, the Teacher
must copy the "A" and "B" prescriptions exactly as he is

<u>SCORING FORM</u>

NAME <u>John Jones</u>   SEQUENCE NO: <u>480</u>
DATE <u>Dec.18, 1970</u>

Scoring: exemptions: <u>4</u>

<u>items</u>

```
[ 1 ][ 2 ][ 3 ][ 4 ][ 5 ][ 6 ][ 7 ][ 8 ][ 9 ][10]
[11][12][13][14][15][16][17][18][19][20]
[21][22][23][24][25][26][27][28][29][30]
[31][32][33][34][35][36][37][38][39][40]
[■■][42][43][44][45][46][47][48][49][50]
[51][52][53][54][55][56][57][58][59][60]
[61][62][63][64][65][66][67][68][69][70]
[71][72][73][74][75][76][77][78][79][80]
[81][82][83][84][85][86][87][88][89][90]
[91][92][93][94][95][96][97][98][99][100]
```

<u>passes</u>

[1][2][3][■][5]

Assignment:

Student gets all items right: <u>485</u>

Student uses up all passes: <u>479</u>

Supervised by: _____

Fig. 9 — A Scoring Form as it would be filled out by a Teacher on the basis of the Teacher
Form in Figure 8.

30

informed by the Teacher Activity Checklist. Furthermore, the decision as to which prescription to assign the Student is not a discretionary matter for the Teacher. This decision is exclusively the result of rigid adherence to the scoring procedures (see Section 2.6) on the part of the Teacher. The scoring procedure, not pedagogical discretion, determines the prescription.

With the Scoring Form thus prepared, as in Figure 9, the Teacher begins his tutoring of the Student. He presents items to be practiced and he keeps track of the Student's performance according to the procedure described in Figure 10.

To summarize the scoring system: The Teacher works his way through a list of items, checking each off by number on the Scoring Form whenever the Student gets it correct <u>and only then</u>. He keeps going through the list, re-presenting items that have not been checked off, until

a)   all the items that need to be checked off (36 out of 40 in Figure 9) are checked off, in which case, the IF "A" case, the Teacher makes the "Student gets enough items right" assignment, or

b)   the stated number of passes through the list has been exhausted, in which case, the IF "B" case, the Teacher makes the "Student uses up all passes" assignment, whichever comes first.

31

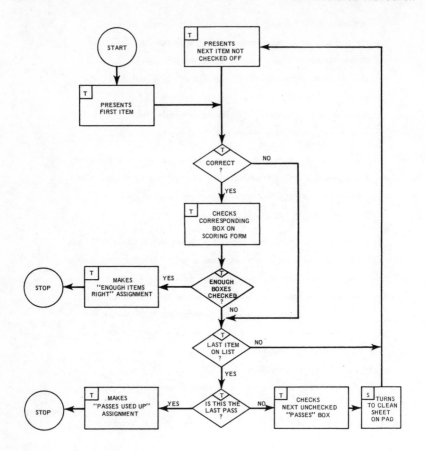

Fig. 10 – The Scoring algorithm observed by Teachers.

32

In essence, the Teacher uses the Scoring Form to keep track of
which items the Student has gotten correct and which iteration through
the list the Student is on. When a Student's performance reaches an
assignment threshold, e.g., the requisite number of boxes have been
checked off, the Teacher observes this and makes the appropriate
assignment.

Possible Questions:

1)   How does the scoring system work? See Section 2.6.

3.0   PMI/MS: Review of Materials and Personnel Functions

3.1   Materials

3.1.1   The Student Activity Checklist (Appendix C) -- for Student use

A student Manual can be assembled in a loose-leaf notebook which
is distributed, one to each student in the class, during the trainee's
initial orientation to PMI/MS. This notebook contains the Student Acitvity
Checklist sheets for a fully worked out sequence of assignments for the
Student to engage in specific learning activities with specific materials.
This book is prepared by the curricular staff responsible for PMI/MS
implementation. (See Section 5.1)

3.1.2   The Teacher Activity Checklist (Appendix D) -- for Teacher use

A loose-leaf notebook, one for each pair of trainees, the Teacher
Activity Checklists contain one entry (Seq. No.) for every supervised
activity assigned in the Student Activity Checklist. The pages of the
Teacher Manual tell the Teacher how to conduct a supervised learning
activity, how to monitor the Student's progress, and how to select
which of two (or more) alternative prescriptions to make based upon
the Student's performance.

33

3.1.3   Scoring Forms (Appendix B, p. B2) -- for Teacher use

Scoring Forms are special work sheets containing a Scoring Field and
an Assignment Field. A Scoring Form is prepared by a Teacher on the basis
of an entry in the Teacher Activity Checklist. Using the prepared Scoring
Form as an aid, the Teacher monitors the progress of his Student. Completed Scoring Forms are filed by Teacher (See Section 4.1.1) and are
preserved as part of the permanent record of trainee achievement.

3.1.4   Reader's Evaluation Forms (Appendix B., p. B3) -- for Student
             use

These are forms on which a student evaluates and writes critical reviews of passages that his Student Manual requires him to read.

3.1.5*   MIND Text (one for each trainee) (Appendix A) -- for Student
             use

3.1.6*   Correct Answer Book (Appendix E) -- for Teacher use

These are either text copies that contain the correct answers (e.g.,
a so-called Teacher's Edition) or a correct answer book specially con-
cocted in the event that the instructional materials lack such special
additions, as did the MIND materials used in the New York Telephone project, (which required the production of an easily prepared, but nonetheless voluminous answer book of 316 one-sided pages).

If the answer book is homemade and bound in a three-ring-loose-leaf
notebook, it is highly advisable to use a Sellmaster binder or its

----

*This component is incidental to PMI/MS. PMI/MS assumes only
that instructional materials of some sort actually exist. Thus, 3.5
and 3.6 could reference any text materials.

equivalent. These notebooks stand open a few degrees off the vertical, facilitating the scoring process and preventing the Student from seeing the correct answers.

If a printed answer book is used, it should be supported by a bookstand.

SPECIAL NOTE: An alternate configuration, but one that has not yet been tested, combines the Teacher Activity Checklist (3.1.2) with the Correct Answer Book (3.1.6) according to the format given in Appendix B-6. The advantage of this configuration could be 1) one less physical component for trainees to manipulate and 2) a slightly lessened materials cost.

3.2   Personnel Functions

3.2.1   The PMI/MS Instructor (See Section 4.4)

The PMI/MS instructor is responsible for the classroom operation of the PMI/MS system.

3.2.2   The PMI/MS Administrator (See Section 4.5)

The administrator is the coordinator of the PMI/MS class as a whole, managing classroom inventory, monitoring trainee performance and trouble shooting for one or several PMI/MS classrooms.

4.0   PMI/MS: Details of Administration

4.1   Facilities

PMI/MS is a system for the classroom; any reasonably fitted out classroom will suffice for its implementation. This classroom should contain the following:

1)   Sufficient table space for pairs of trainees to sit across
      from one another comfortably. The arm room separating one
      pair from the next should be adequate. 3' x 6' is the
      minimum table dimension for two pairs; 3' x 8' or 3' x 10'
      would be better.

      The New York Telephone configuration is shown in Figure
      11. The facilities were designed to accommodate classes of
      12-13 trainees.

2)   A storage area (e.g., a book shelf) to house one Teacher
      Activity Checklist for each Student-Teacher pair, one Student
      Activity Checklist for each trainee, for texts and other
      materials, and for answer books and, if necessary, bookstands.

3)   A forms file (a paper accordian file sequenced alphabetically)
      in which Students will file completed Reader's Evaluation Forms
      and Teachers will file completed Scoring Forms. (How often
      are the contents of this file removed? See Section 4.4.)

Needless to say, the entire facility should be well-lit and ventilated,
and should be as free from distractions as possible (e.g., a minimum of
visitors to class).

4.2   Procedures for Pairing Trainees

4.2.1   Basic Constraints

Although many different pairing procedures are possible, all procedures, if they are to work well, must take careful note of one major
consideration. Trainees should not understand any pairings to be permanent,
that is, to be valid for any longer than a PMI/MS session. The reason is

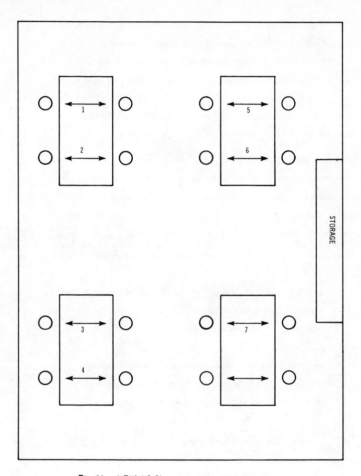

Fig. 11 – A PMI/MS Classroom at New York Telephone

37

this: A PMI/MS instructor will rapidly become sensitive to nuances of
pairing and will want to manipulate pairings upon occasion on a discretionary basis. If the trainee has become accustomed to permanence in
pairing, i.e., to a particular partner, it will become that much harder
for the instructor to make pairing changes. The pairing procedure must
create a psychology in which daily change of partners is accepted as
the rule and not as the exception.

The best pairing procedure will involve an element of chance, for
the most changeful environment is one in which events are apparently
random occurrences, acts of Fate. What such an environment tells the
trainee is that he can't and does not need to anticipate working with
the same person tomorrow that he is working with today.

Procedures of this type solve many problems, in addition to the
primary one.

1) From the point of view of the trainee, pairings even with
   a personally objectionable partner are tolerable because
   it's only for one day. Tomorrow, chances are, each will
   have a new partner.

2) From the point of view of the trainer, random pairing
   simulates the on-the-job atmosphere where a multiplicity
   of relationships with all kinds of people is the rule
   rather than the exception.

The pairing procedure used in the New York Telephone project was
linked to the configuration of the classroom (See Figure 11). At the
beginning of each PMI/MS session, trainees would draw from a "hat" containing chips; two 1's, two 2's, two 3's, two 4's, two 5's, two 6's,

and a blank (which was not used on days when there was an even number of
trainees in the class). A trainee would take one of the two positions
at the peer-location designated by the chip. Another trainee would ultimately draw the second chip with the same peer-position indicated, and
thus a peer pair would be formed for the day.

4.2.2   The Role-Swap

At exactly the half-way point in each PMI/MS session, trainees
should swap roles. The former Teacher relinquishes control of the
Correct Answer Book and the Teacher Activity Checklist to the new
Teacher and opens up his own Student Activity Checklist. The former
Student closes up his Student Manual and takes over Teaching responsi-
bilities as he may be requested by the new Student.

4.2.3   Dealing with the Odd-Man Situation

If the class has an odd number of trainees, as it is quite likely
to have on any particular day, it becomes necessary to provide teaching services for the odd-man in his role as Student. The most natural
source is the pool of Teachers in down-time. (See Section 4.3). At
any particular moment, there will be some Teachers whose services are
not needed by their Students, for these Students will be involved in
independent activities. If the odd-man needs a Teacher, the instructor
should summon one from the ranks of the Teachers in down-time. This
Teacher should work with the odd-man for one supervised activity. The
instructor should then summon another Teacher, if needed.

4.2.4   Grouping Considerations

A random pairing procedure of the sort recommended in Section 4.2
can founder if it results in a pairing of two trainees who are widely

divergent in aptitude and/or performance. Two trainees who represent
such extreme polarities can and possibly will lose patience with one
another. Thus, such pairing should be avoided wherever possible.
There are two approaches to this problem, one to take prior to the
start of the course and one to take in the event that pairing problems
arise once the course has commenced. Both approaches involve grouping the trainees.

4.2.4.1   Initial Grouping

When trainees are apportioned to different classrooms and/or
instructors, they should be grouped on the basis of ability <u>with respect
to the syllabus to be taught</u>, that is, on the basis of a simple pretest
whose items are drawn in sequence from the instructional materials
to be used; in fact, the pretest should be a final "criterion" test
in miniature; it could be a ten or fifteen minute timed test on vocabulary words selected comprehensively from the instructional materials,
i.e., a criterion test used for diagnostic purposes. This will insure
that the trainees in particular classes will be more or less equivalent
with respect to their advance knowledge of the subject matter. Even
such pretesting is not foolproof, however, for it does not take motivation into account.

4.2.4.2   Sub-Grouping During PMI/MS Operations

It can emerge, as it did in one of the three classes of the New York
Telephone study, that some trainees will progress extremely rapidly and
others will progress extremely slowly. (In the New York Telephone study,
trainees differed in rate of progress at one time by as much as a factor
of 4.) The easiest thing to do should this situation arise <u>and</u> appear to

cause problems is to sub-group the class into two groups, two sub-classes
in effect, on the basis of learning rate. (How are such records kept? See
Section 4.5) The random pairing procedure should then be applied daily
to each sub-class separately. Thus, it will thereafter appear that a
single classroom is running two different PMI/MS classes simultaneously.

4.3   Teacher Down-time

Depending upon the size of the ratio of independent activities to
supervised activities, the Teacher will, to a greater or lesser extent,
have time when his services are not needed. If the Student spends half
of his time on independent activities, then it follows that his Teacher
will be free for half of the time.

In the New York Telephone study, Teacher down-time was handled in
two ways.

1)   Teachers in down-time were permitted to study ahead in their
      texts.

2)   Also, each classroom contained a small library of up-to-date
      paperback books, and could well include job related materials.
      Teachers in down-time could read these books if they wanted to,
      on a first-come first-serve basis. Trainees were encouraged
      to take these books home, but were asked to bring them back
      each day so that the entire library was available for Teachers
      in down-time.

3)   Teachers in down-time were subject to the instructor's request
      to work with the odd man, if he existed. (See Section 4.2.3.)

4.4   <u>What the PMI/MS Instructor Does</u>

Provides student orientation to PMI/MS. (See Section 4.4.1)

Administers and Maintains PMI/MS. (See Section 4.4.2)

Answers questions of relating procedure and course content.

Counsels students.

Adjudicates disputes.

Maintains trainee records. (See Section 4.4.3)

4.4.1   <u>Trainee Orientation to PMI/MS</u>

Orientation to PMI/MS falls under the jurisdiction of the instructor
and it is perhaps the most crucial event in the running of PMI/MS, for it
is at this time that the trainee is going to acquire his first attitudes
toward the PMI/MS system.

The orientation process is a very idiosyncratic one for instructors.
We have observed some who have given a two-session blackboard presentation
on PMI/MS before ever introducing trainees to the materials -- <u>a don't
touch</u> orientation. On the other extreme, we have seen others introduce
trainees to the procedures via <u>hands-on</u> experience almost from the outset,
providing orientation by demonstrating, giving practice, and by correcting.
Both of these approaches, which differ quite markedly in terms of certain
distinctions, appear to work for PMI/MS. So do many other approaches. By
far, the most important factors seem to be that the instructor should fully
understand PMI/MS himself and that he should be given free reign to conceive
an orientation approach that suits his personal approach to teaching.

In any event, an orientation should accomplish what would be the
effects of the following steps.

42

1)   Trainees are given an <u>overview of PMI/MS</u>, emphasizing the
     role-playing aspect of the system -- that trainees are
     either Teachers or Students <u>all of the time that the</u>
     <u>system is in use.</u>

2)   The instructor then explains the <u>pairing procedure</u> and the
     daily selection routine. (See Section 4.2)

3)   With the help of the trainees, the instructor moves the class-
     room furniture into its PMI/MS organization and, then,
     runs through the pairing procedure with the trainees.

4)   Materials are distributed.

     All trainees receive a Student Activity Checklist and tests
     (e.g., MIND). Each position (seven in Figure 11) receives a
     Teacher Activity Checklist and a Correct Answer Book.
     Trainees are introduced to Reader Evaluation Forms and Scor-
     ing Forms without explanation, and are shown where they
     will be located.

5)   The instructor then introduces trainees to the Student role,
     explaining the use of the Student Activity Checklist (see
     Section 3.1), the materials that are addressed by that Check-
     list (see Section 3.5), and the Reader's Evaluation Forms
     (see Section 3.4).

6)   The instructor next explains the Teacher role, making
     explicit reference to the Teacher Activity Checklist (see
     Section 3.2), the Correct Answer Book (see Section 3.6),
     the Scoring Form (see Section 3.3), and the procedures
     associated with its use (see Sections 2.5-2.6).

7)   The instructor now initiates PMI/MS practice in which the
role assignment procedure is employed and trainees work
with the PMI/MS orientation materials (see Section 4.7.2).
The instructor answers procedural questions and corrects
deviations from acceptable PMI/MS procedures (the frequency
of which will diminish noticeably during the first few PMI/MS
sessions).

SPECIAL NOTE: Instructors with no previous PMI/MS experience can be misled
into believing that the system is working when in fact it is not
by the mere appearance of the classroom. Trainees may give the
appearance of working diligently with each other; but on closer
inspection, the Teacher in this or that pair turns out not to be
scoring correctly or not to be presenting items correctly. It generally takes several hours of careful supervision on the part of the
instructor to insure that the system is working correctly for all trainees.

4.4.2   Administration and Maintenance

The daily administrational routine is a very simple one, consisting
of the following steps.

1)   The instructor performs the daily pairing. (See Section 4.2)

2)   The instructor figures out the half-way point in time, the time
of the role-swap, and posts this time on the blackboard. (If
time is to be taken out for breaks, the length of the break time
must be taken into account when the calculation is performed.)

3) The instructor clears out the forms file (See Section 4.1)
at the end of each session.

The few <u>maintenance</u> items on the system are these.

1) Instructors should continually spot-check to make sure that
the Teaching procedures have not been diluted through the
inventiveness of the trainees.

2) The supply of Reader Evaluation Forms and Scoring Forms
should be replenished as needed.

3) The correct answer materials should be kept current by the
instructor with trainee progress.

The one aspect of PMI/MS management that demands diligence and discretion on the part of the classroom instructor and that aspect is the
maintenance of the PMI/MS peer mediation procedures. Unless the instructor
insists that these procedures be maintained by the trainees, the trainees
themselves will, understandably, tend to dilute these procedures to the
point of ineffectiveness. Particularly in regard to the scoring procedures
described in Section 2.5 and 2.6 is this an important consideration. On
the other hand, it may well turn out that certain of the interactive procedures specified in the PMI/MS design for particular exercises will appear
to a greater or lesser extent to be irrelevant to the successful achievement of the instructional goals overall. In certain of these instances,
the instructor, may reasonably permit these procedures to be relaxed.

4.4.3   The Keeping of Trainee Records

The performance of a PMI/MS system in progress can be monitored
and measured quite accurately, and hence controlled (see Section 4.5
and 4.6), providing that certain specific trainee records are maintained.
The most useful record to keep -- indeed, an instructor would be
lost without it -- is the daily sequence number progress of each trainee.
Recording these data on a daily basis and in a form suitable for use
is the responsibility of the instructor. And the basic document
produced by the instructor is the Progress Chart of supervised activities
(the Progress Chart). A hypothetical version of this chart including the
MIND material in Appendix A appears in Figure 12.

Once a day, or after each PMI/MS session, the instructor empties
the Forms File and logs for each trainee the activities that each trainee
has been checked off on during the just completed session. The instructor
dates the first such activity done on that day, and then checks all
sebsequent activities done on that day.

In this way, the basic data of trainee progress are recorded.

4.5   The PMI/MS Administrator Does

Exercises responsibility for instructor preparedness. (See
Section 4.7.1)

Maintains classroom inventory   (See Section 3.1)

Monitors PMI/MS operations (See Section 4.9)

Troubleshoots.

46

Lesson Units Completed

	20	40	50	70	110	120	130	140	180	190	200	250	260	270	310	320	330	340	360	370	380	385	390	400	440	450	460	470	480	500	510	530
HORN, ABRAHAM	2/29	√	√	√	√	√	√	√	√	√	√	√	√	√	√	√	√	√	√	√	√	√	√	√	√	√	√	√	2/30	√	√	√
FORMAN, GEORGE	2/29	√	√	√	√	√	√	√	√	√	√	√	√	√	√	√	√	√	√	√	√	√	√	√	√	√	√	√	√	√	√	√
RIVERA, RAFAEL	2/29	√	√	√	√	√	√	√	√	√	√	√	√	√	√	√	√	√	√	√	√	√	√	√	√	√	2/30	√	√	√	√	√
TOBIN, JOHN	2/29	√	√	√	√	√	√	√	√	√	√	√	√	√	√	√	√	√	√	√	√	√	√	√	√	√	√	√	√	√	√	√
CINIGLIO, VINCENT	2/29	√	√	√	√	√	√	√	√	√	√	√	√	√	√	√	√	√	√	√	√	√	√	√	√	√	√	√	√	√	√	√
ENGEL, FRANK	2/29	√	√	√	√	√	√	√	√	√	√	√	√	√	√	√	√	√	√	√	√	√	√	√	√	√	√	√	√	√	2/30	√
GREENBAUM, CHARLES	2/29	√	√	√	√	√	√	√	√	√	√	√	√	√	√	√	√	√	2/30	√	√	√	√	√	√	√	√	√	√	√	√	√
LEWIS, ROBERT	2/29	√	√	√	√	√	√	√	√	√	√	√	√	√	√	√	√	√	√	√	√	√	√	√	√	√	√	√	√	√	√	√
TORRES, JOSE	2/29	√	√	√	√	√	√	√	√	√	√	√	√	√	√	√	√	√	2/30	√	√	√	√	√	√	√	√	√	√	√	√	√
MULLIGAN, DONALD	2/29	√	√	√	√	√	√	√	√	√	√	√	√	√	√	√	√	√	√	√	√	√	√	√	√	√	√	√	√	√	√	√
SMITH, ALLAN	2/29	√	√	√	√	√	√	√	√	√	√	√	√	√	√	√	√	√	√	√	√	√	√	√	√	√	√	√	√	√	√	√
STAPLETON, EDWARD	2/29	√	√	√	√	√	√	√	√	√	√	√	√	√	√	√	√	√	√	√	√	√	√	√	√	√	√	√	√	√	√	√
SEXTON, JOSEPH	2/29	√	√	√	√	√	√	√	√	√	√	√	√	√	√	√	√	√	√	√	√	√	√	√	√	√	√	√	√	√	√	√
O'NEILL, ANTHONY	2/29	√	√	√	√	√	√	√	√	√	√	√	√	√	√	√	√	√	√	√	√	√	√	√	√	√	√	√	√	√	√	√
McCABE, MICHAEL	2/29	√	√	√	√	√	√	√	√	√	√	√	√	√	√	√	√	√	√	√	√	√	√	√	√	√	√	√	√	√	√	√
MARK, SIDNEY	2/29	√	√	√	√	√	√	√	√	√	√	√	√	√	√	√	√	√	√	√	√	√	√	√	√	√	√	√	√	√	√	√
SANTIAGO, PABLO	2/29	√	√	√	√	√	√	√	√	√	√	√	√	√	√	√	√	√	√	√	√	√	√	√	√	√	√	√	√	√	√	√
AVILES, MIGUEL	2/29	√	√	√	√	√	√	√	√	√	√	√	√	√	√	√	√	√	√	√	√	√	√	√	√	√	√	√	√	√	√	√
FITZGERALD, HUGH	2/29	√	√	√	√	√	√	√	√	√	√	√	√	√	√	√	√	√	√	√	√	√	√	√	√	√	√	√	√	√	√	√
GOREN, JOEL	2/29	√	√	√	√	√	√	√	√	√	√	√	√	√	√	√	√	√	√	√	√	√	√	√	√	√	√	√	√	√	√	√
KENT, FELIX	2/29	√	√	√	√	√	√	√	√	√	√	√	√	√	√	√	√	√	√	√	√	√	√	√	√	√	√	√	√	√	√	√
GRIFFIN, DENNIS	2/29	√	√	√	√	√	√	√	√	√	√	√	√	√	√	√	√	√	√	√	√	√	√	√	√	√	√	√	√	√	√	√
GOLDSMITH, CURT	2/29	√	√	√	√	√	√	√	√	√	√	√	√	√	√	√	√	√	√	√	√	√	√	√	√	√	√	√	√	√	√	√
DOOLEY, JASON	2/29	√	√	√	√	√	√	√	√	√	√	√	√	√	√	√	√	√	√	√	√	√	√	√	√	√	√	√	√	√	√	√
MORSE, RICHARD	2/29	√	√	√	√	√	√	√	√	√	√	√	√	√	√	√	√	√	√	√	√	√	√	√	√	√	√	√	√	√	√	√
KRASILOUSKY, MIKE	2/29	√	√	√	√	√	√	√	√	√	√	√	√	√	√	√	√	√	√	√	√	√	√	√	√	√	√	√	√	√	√	√
SADLER, RALPH	2/29	√	√	√	√	√	√	√	√	√	√	√	√	√	√	√	√	√	√	√	√	√	√	√	√	√	√	√	√	√	√	√
TIMMINS, LAWRENCE	2/29	√	√	√	√	√	√	√	√	√	√	√	√	√	√	2/30	√	√	√	√	√	√	√	√	√	√	√	√	√	√	√	√
ROLLIN, LEON	2/29	√	√	√	√	√	√	√	√	√	√	√	√	√	√	√	√	√	√	√	√	√	√	√	√	√	√	√	√	√	√	√
CURLEY, JOHN	2/29	√	√	√	√	√	√	√	√	√	√	√	√	√	√	√	√	√	√	√	√	√	√	√	√	√	√	√	√	√	√	√
MARCUS, MAURICE	2/29	√	√	√	√	√	√	√	√	√	√	√	√	√	√	√	√	√	√	√	√	√	√	√	√	√	√	√	√	√	√	√
BUBA, DOMINICK	2/29	√	√	√	√	√	√	√	√	√	√	√	√	√	√	√	√	√	√	√	√	√	√	√	√	√	√	√	√	√	√	√
VEGA, JUAN	2/29	√	√	√	√	√	√	√	√	√	√	√	√	√	√	√	√	√	√	√	√	√	√	√	√	√	√	√	√	√	√	√
WILLIAMS, JORDAN	2/29	√	√	√	√	√	√	√	√	√	√	√	√	√	√	√	√	√	√	√	√	√	√	√	√	√	√	√	√	√	√	√
ZEFF, ARTHUR	2/29	√	√	√	√	√	√	√	√	√	√	√	√	√	√	√	√	√	√	√	√	√	√	√	√	√	√	√	√	√	√	√
KATZ, BENJAMIN	2/29	√	√	√	√	√	√	√	√	√	√	√	√	√	√	√	√	√	√	√	√	√	√	√	√	√	√	√	√	√	√	√
DWYER, CORNELIUS	2/29	√	√	√	√	√	√	√	√	√	√	√	√	√	√	√	√	√	√	√	√	√	√	√	√	√	√	√	√	√	√	√
PADRO, RAFAEL	2/29	√	√	√	√	√	√	√	√	√	√	√	√	√	√	√	√	√	√	√	√	√	√	√	√	√	√	√	√	√	√	√

Fig. 12 – Progress Chart of Supervised Learning Activities Completed (Simulated)

4.6   Criterion Testing

    A criterion test is a test of subject matter mastery, a measure
of extent, of how well a person has learned what the instructional
system has intended him to learn. Such tests should be included in all
instructional programs. Scores generated by such tests are valuable not
only for measuring the performance of trainees with respect to the program they are in; they are essential to determining whether a planned
(or unplanned) change in the PMI/MS system or the set of materials
operating under it has been an improvement or a mistake.

    Criterion tests can most easily be entered into the PMI/MS sequence
of Student activities, that is, by making the test activity, a PMI/MS
Student activity.

    In the language skills, short, timed criterion tests (e.g., 20 minutes)
are generally satisfactory.

4.7   Start-up Guidelines

4.7.1   If PMI/MS is being introduced into a training environment for
the first time, care should be taken to switch over from the conventional
management system to PMI/MS under optimal conditions.

    1)   Instructors should be thoroughly familiar with PMI/MS prior
           to the start of the training cycle. An orientation period,
           lasting two days, should be provided for new instructors during
           which they should carefully study this manual, ask questions
           of someone knowledgeable about the system, and engage in
           PMI/MS simulations in the roles of Teachers and Student.

2)   Time should be allowed prior to the start of PMI/MS for trainees to become familiar with the school/job environment, to know something about their instructors and the authority structure within which the instructors operate, and merely to have had the experience of having survived for a few days in the school context.

In the typical 5-day-a-week schedule of the industrial training environment, these conditions can generally be satisfied by the beginning of the second week of a cycle. The decision to start PMI/MS at any <u>particular</u> time must be made only by the instructor.

If the instructor has had previous experience with PMI/MS, then, of course, PMI/MS orientation for trainees could probably begin even during the first week of instruction.

4.7.2   The designer of the PMI/MS syllabus must be certain that the early Student assignments, the ones that will be used during the <u>trainee orientation phase,</u> (see Section 4.4.1), are so simple that everyone in the class can get through them easily. The early content of the PMI/MS learning activities should be easily understood by all of the trainees, which is to say, the trainees should not be distracted by issues of content while learning the operating procedure of PMI/MS.

We recommend that the syllabus designer employ <u>two to four</u> hours of such PMI/MS material for use during the trainee orientation period.

49

4.7.3   PMI/MS provides <u>completely</u> individualized pacing, a fact that
has great practical significance for a classroom undergoing conversion
from a conventional time-paced (lock-step) system of management to PMI/MS.
For it would quickly be observed that, under PMI/MS, most if not all
traineeswill complete the work sequence sooner, some a great deal sooner,
than the former schedule would have dictated. This time-to-completion
difference between the new and old systems is not a particularly important
problem if remedial language instruction is the entire curriculum. PMI/MS
trainees will simply complete the course sooner. However, if for practical
reasons, a trainee simply cannot be discharged from the school as soon
as he has completed the reading component of instruction, e.g., as when
the curriculum contains other necessary but time-paced subjects, it will
then become necessary (and instructionally desirable) to supply supplementary
reading experiences. If the trainee himself is permitted to select the
supplementary reading (perhaps from an extensive list of options, he will
look forward with some anticipation toward the completion of the PMI/MS
component of the course). Finishing PMI/MS will take on additional meaning
and priority as an accomplishment.

4.8   <u>PMI/MS Operations Chronology</u>

4.8.1   Prior to the commencement of the use of PMI/MS in a particular
classroom:

1)   The classroom instructor receives PMI/MS orientation (required
     only in the case of instructors with no previous PMI/MS experience).

50

2)   The instructor establishes facilities. (See Section 4.1.)

3)   The instructor gets and prepares for use all PMI/MS materials
     from the curriculum planning specialist. (See Sections 3.0-3.7.)

4)   The instructor constructs a Progress Chart. (See Section 4.4.3.)

4.8.2   Upon the commencement of PMI/MS use, which might come on the
very first day of the entire course of instruction or at a later date, the
instructor initiates the trainee orientation cycle. (See Section 4.4.1.)

4.9   Charts and Graphs of Use in Monitoring PMI/MS Operations

4.9.1   The Progress Histogram

     This graph, an example of which appears in Figure 13, expresses
student progress as a wave, where the peaks represent the position of greatest number of students and the low points, the position of the fewest.
Overlapping histograms can be drawn at convenient and meaningful intervals,
over a week perhaps, to reflect class progress over time.

     The progress histogram is simply a summary of total class progress.
This histogram itself is generated by examining the Progress Chart (Figure 12)
to determine how many trainees ended up in a given and predetermined range
of sequence numbers and then by plotting these frequencies.

5.0   PMI/MS Designing Your Own

     The central act in the design of a PMI/MS implementation is an act
of instructional systems engineering. It involves

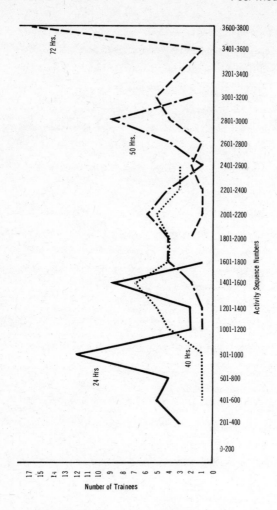

Fig. 13 – Progress Histogram from NYT Study (Four Overlapping
Graphs Drawn 24, 40, 55, and 72 Hours of PMI/MS Instruction).

1)   selecting and sequencing instructional content,

2)   inventing interactive learning activities

3)   establishing scoring thresholds (e.g., number of exemptions)

4)   assembling PMI/MS materials.

5.1   Starting Out

The quality of PMI/MS implementations is related, not surprisingly, to the experience of the designer. The best initial experience would be for the designer to use the body of this manual as a textbook, and to use the appendix material as a problem to be worked out. Appendices C and D are Student and Teacher Manuals based upon the content of the text material in Appendix A. Appendix E contains the correct answer for these materials. The PMI/MS syllabus designer should work with the text and appendices together until he is absolutely certain that he understands how the New York Telephone syllabus designers designed Appendices C and D on the basis of Appendix A. He should observe how:

Sections of MIND units such as "Skill Group C" were resectioned for assignment by the Teacher Manual. The only criterion used was one of estimated duration. The designers of this sample did not want any supervised learning activity, a certain amount of unproductive overhead time goes into getting started (by Teacher and Student) and finishing up. One technique, therefore, of maximizing the overall productivity of PMI/MS in a particular implementation is to keep the overhead time to a minimum in relation to productive instructional time. Thus, the designer should prefer long (20 minute) activities to short (5 minute) ones.

The Student Activity Checklist must state very precisely the exact location of the work to be performed. If it is not precise, the instructor will be plagued by questions that could have been pre-answered.

Note that as many MIND activities as possible were converted to supervised activities, this so as to achieve the full potential of the PMI/MS technique.

Care must be taken on the Teacher Activity Checklists.

1) The sequence number correspondence with the sequence numbers of the Student Activity Checklist must be exact.

2) The designer <u>can</u> override the procedures in a text via the Procedures field on the Student and Teacher Forms. When he does this, the designer must be sure to state his own procedures very precisely.

3) Careful thought needs to be given to how many times a Student ought to be permitted to go through a list of items of a certain type before he is to be directed to a remedial assignment or even to the instructor for special assistance.

4) The designer should observe the technique whereby advanced sequence numbers can refer to assignments previously performed, (See Appendix C, p. 3, seq. No. 479). He should recognize how this technique permits a Student to be branched to a previously performed page in the textbook without his having thereupon to do all of this activities intervening in the Student Activity Checklist to re-attain his place. (See Appendix C, C7, C14, C15).

In summary, anyone who, having studied this manual, can understand how Appendix C and Appendix D relate to Appendix A is capable in principle of designing and implementing a version of PMI/MS.

The central fact to keep in mind is that this manual is partially tailored for the MIND materials. Thus it is not the specific details of this particular MIND-based system that are crucial, but the basic elements of PMI/MS systems in general as they emerge from this implementation.

5.2   The Necessary Materials

1)   A supply of blank Student Activity Checklists.

2)   A supply of blank Teacher Activity Checklists.

3)   A supply of Correct Answer Forms (if called for).

4)   An accounting and inventory of all instructional materials that would be available to PMI/MS students.

5.3   The Use of Sequence Numbers

Sequence numbers should be assigned in tens rather than units in the Student Activity Checklist so as to facilitate the updating of the Checklist by interleaving new activities with the old.

5.4   Updating the Syllabus

It may occur with fair frequency that a curricular decision will be made to add, delete, or rearrange material in a PMI/MS syllabus. Care should be taken, in such cases, to insure that new material is sequenced

correctly with respect to the old material and that the duration of the
new activity falls within the range that exists for the old activities.

A1

Appendix A

A Sample from a Text (MIND)

A2

WORD ATTACK SKILLS

Building Words with a Suffix

SECTION 1

--Some words have a suffix. A <u>suffix</u> is a group

of letters that can be added at the <u>end</u> of a word.

An example of a suffix is "ĭng." You can add

the suffix "ing" to the word "hopé" to make "hōping."

--Circle all of the words that end with a suffix.

hating	baking	wed	rate	yell
hog	hopping	raving	rope	drawing
make	sagging	beg	telling	

SECTION 2

--To add the suffix "ing" to a word that ends with

silent "e," drop the "e" and add "ing."

EXAMPLE: datė + ing = dāt + ĭng = dātĭng

--Work with your group to do 3 things to the following

words:

1)   Pronounce each word;

2)   Mark all the vowels; and

3)   Add the suffix "ing."

58

A3

crave -----c̄rȧvĭng   drive -----_____

tame -----_____   fake -----_____

rise -----_____   vote -----_____

save -----_____   tune -----_____

bake -----_____   wave -----_____

SECTION 3

--Work by yourself to do 3 things to the following words:

1)   Pronounce each one;

2)   Mark the vowels; and

3)   Add the suffix "ing."

rūle-----r̄ūlĭng   fade-----_____

date-----_____   wipe-----_____

pave-----_____   stake----_____

bale-----_____   rise-----_____

tune-----_____   note-----_____

--Check your answers with your group and your monitor.

SECTION 4

--To add the suffix "ing" to a short vowel word, you

must have 2 consonants before adding "ing."

--If a short vowel word already ends with 2 consonants,

just add "ing."

EXAMPLE: trĭck + ĭng = trĭckĭng

59

A4

--Work with your group to do 3 things to the

following words:

    1)   Pronounce each one;

    2)   Underline the consonants at the end of

        the word; and

    3)   Add the suffix "ing."

lick-----licking_____   pick-----_____

sell -----_____   truck----_____

stack----_____   pack-----_____

pull-----_____   mock----_____

SECTION 5

--Work by yourself to do 4 things to the following

words:

    1)   Pronounce each one;

    2)   Mark the vowels;

    3)   Underline the consonants the word ends

        with; and

    4)   Add the suffix "ing."

pick-----_picking_____   bill-----_____

dock-----_____   stalk----_____

tell-----_____   will-----_____

rock----_____   lock-----_____

fall-----_____   buck-----_____

--Check your answers with your group or monitor

A5

SECTION 6

--You already know that to add the suffix "ing" to a

short vowel word, the word must end with 2

consonants.

--So, if a short vowel word ends with only 1 consonant,

add another one like the last one, then add "ing."

EXAMPLE: bĕg + g + ĭng = bĕggĭng

--Work with your group to do 4 things to the following

words:

    1)   Pronounce each one;

    2)   Mark the vowels;

    3)   Double the last consonant; ånd

    4)   Add the suffix "ing."

lĕt----- lĕttĭng   spot-----_____

scan----_____   dig------_____

snap----_____   hog------_____

snag----_____   mob-----_____

wet-----_____   rot-----_____

61

A6

SECTION 7   --Work by yourself to do 4 things to the following words:

    1)   Pronounce each one;

    2)   Mark the vowels;

    3)   Underline the consonant the word ends

        with, and

    4)   Add the suffix "ing."

păn------pănnĭng	chop----- _____
nag------ _____	tan------ _____
trap----- _____	sun----- _____
cut------ _____	snip---- _____
mop----- _____	grab--- _____

--Check your answers with your group and your monitor.

SECTION 8   --The following list contains both long vowel words and

short vowel words. Work by yourself to do 3 things to

the following words:

    1)   Pronounce each one;

    2)   Mark the vowels; and

    3)   Add the suffix "ing."

bĕg----- bĕggĭng	pack-------- _____
set----- _____	strip------- _____
wade--- _____	mop------- _____
gĕt----- _____	smell------ _____

62

A7

lock----_____   tan--------_____

save----_____   park------_____

chat----_____   fade------_____

--Check your answers with your group and your

monitor.

SECTION 9   --The part of a word to which you add the suffix

has a name. It is called a "root." By adding suffixes

to a root, you can make words grow just like a

tree grows from its roots.

EXAMPLE: Word-with-a-suffix   Root   Suffix

nĕckĭng   =   nĕck   +   ĭng

hōpĭng   =   hōpe̸   +   ĭng

hŏppĭng   =   hŏp   +   ĭng

--Work as a group to do 3 things to the following

words:

1)   Pronounce each one;

2)   Mark the vowels; and

3)   Find the root word.

pĕckĭng-----__pĕck_   spanning-----_____

filling------_____   snagging-----_____

docking-----_____   trapping-----_____

stalking-----_____   cutting-----_____

63

A8

telling------_____   mopping----_____

ruling------_____   fading------_____

dating------_____   wiping-----_____

paving------_____

SECTION 10   --Work by yourself to do 3 things to the following

words:

1)   Pronounce each one;

2)   Mark the vowels; and

3)   Find the root word.

hŏppĭng-------___hŏp___   biting-------_____

hoping--------_____   letting------_____

lacking-------_____   tanning-----_____

SECTION 11   --Now that you have learned what a suffix is and what a

root word is, look for them in everything you read.

You will find that you have hundreds of new words in

your vocabulary.

A9

VOCABULARY SKILLS

I

allow (al-low') to permit—My mother will allow me to have the party.

ask (ask) to inquire—We will let them ask twenty questions.

attempt (at-tempt') to try—They made a poor attempt and failed.

beat (beat) to hit repeatedly—He was known to beat his wife.

certain (cer'-tain) sure—Are you certain of the facts?

circle (cir'-cle) perfectly round shape—It is hard to draw a good circle freehand.

clean (clean) not dirty—Our new car is clean.

condition (con-di'-tion) state—This room is in an awful condition.

country (coun'-try) areas of land away from big cities—We like to go to the country on weekends.

degree (de-gree') unit of measure of angles—A circle has 360 degrees.

demand (de-mand') to request strongly—I demand my rights.

desire (de-sire') to wish—What sort of work do you really desire?

east (east) the direction of sunrise—The East Coast faces the Atlantic.

gentle (gen'-tle) soft and mild—She said it was gentle soap.

home (home) where you live—My home is across town.

larger (larg'-er) bigger—An elephant is larger than a mouse.

light (light) illumination—The sun gives off light and heat.

lose (lose) to be defeated—Try not to lose this game.

measure (meas'-ure) to find length or weight—Measure the board to find its length.

minute (min'-ute) 1/60th of an hour—There are sixty seconds in one minute.

offer (of'-fer) to suggest—Did she offer any ideas?

pleasure (pleas'-ure) good feeling—The meal gave me great pleasure.

practice (prac'-tice) to perform or work at repeatedly—To do something well requires a lot of practice.

produce (pro-duce') to bring forth—The workers were able to produce more with better lighting.

proper (prop'-er) can mean really good or correct—I'm going to give him a proper whipping.

question (ques'-tion) to inquire or ask—The lawyer was allowed to question the witness.

refuse (re-fuse') to reject—Please do not refuse my suggestion.

remove (re-move') to take away—Soap and water will remove dirt.

require (re-quire') to demand—I require you to finish your work.

sea (sea) ocean—To recover from his illness, he took a long sea voyage.

seek (seek) to search—They seek the missing treasure in the sunken ship.

A10

several (sev'-er-al) more than two, but not very many—Mary has several hats.

smoking (smok'-ing) to give out smoke—The chimney is smoking.

soil (soil) dirt—The soil was dug with a shovel.

strike (strike) to hit—Strike the ball with the bat.

suggest (sug-gest') to hint—I suggest you comb your untidy hair.

suit (suit) a number of things used together—That is a well-made suit of clothes.

uncle (un'-cle) the brother of one's father or mother—My uncle is my mother's brother.

view (view) to see—To view the Grand Canyon is a wonderful experience.

wild (wild) uncontrollable—These children act like wild animals.

SKILL GROUP C

READING SKILLS

PAR. 33-54

33   I want you to take a good look at me. I used to be a happy man. Now I am confused and sad. If you'll just sit here with me for a few minutes, I'll tell you my story.

34   It all began one night when I came home from work. I had hardly gotten beyond the front door when my wife, Alice, came rushing in from the living room and gave me a big kiss. I didn't even have time to take off my hat and coat. Naturally, I was surprised and could only say, "Alice, is anything wrong with the new car? Really, you can tell me."

35   She patted my cheek and smiled, "Everything is fine, dear. Just sit down and rest until dinner is ready. You must be tired from the way you work all day." She handed me the newspaper and went to the kitchen. Now, unless something is wrong, I'm doing well if I get a wave from the hall when I come in. So I shouted, "If your Uncle George is coming for a visit, I'm flying south for the winter!" The only answer was silence.

36   Alice didn't say anything special for a few days, but I could tell that her mind

was busy. Whatever her plan was, and I was sure there was a plan, the children must have been in on it, too. The whole family suddenly acted as if I were the President, or at least a general. My son, John, washed the car at least three times over the week-end and didn't even ask to use it. And his sister, our six-year-old, was as sweet as sugar. She went to bed without a fight, kept her room clean, and said "please" and "thank you" at the table. Usually, she's as wild as an Indian.

37   Furthermore, my wife pressed my suits without my asking; and when I wanted to write a letter, she offered to type it for me. Everyone spoke in a low voice and called me "sir." There was no doubt that something was up.

38   Now, it's hard for me to take strange behavior from my family. I began to look a bit worn and shaky from the strain of worrying about what they were up to. They must have noticed and realized that their plan was a success. All I could do was wait for them to strike! Then one night out of a clear blue sky, it happened. Alice said, "Henry, don't you think it would be a good idea to look into buying a house—maybe one in the

All

country where the children could have room to play?"

39   I believe I should have put up a proper fight right then. Yet, they say you can't beat City Hall and my family is like City Hall, complete with mayor and councilmen. Also, I'm a soft touch. When my wife wants something she looks at me with those soft, brown eyes of hers and, well, it would take a stronger man than me to refuse. I agreed, but only on the condition that she do all the looking and I do the deciding. I felt safe under those conditions.

40   But not for long! Within four days my wife had found the house of her dreams. From that moment on I didn't get a minute's peace. First, I had to hear how wonderful the house was. It was just the size we wanted, had good light, and stood on a hill overlooking a valley below. "Gorgeous view," she said, "and it is cool in the summer because several big shade trees spread their branches over the roof."

41   The yard was big enough to plant a garden to raise fresh flowers for the house. The driveway ran the whole length of the yard and made a circle in back so you didn't have to back the car out. The children could walk to school. There were all sorts of school clubs for them to join in order to develop their talents. Alice promised that it wouldn't take me more than one hour to drive to work.

42   I should mention that I can get to work in five minutes from our present house. And in winter I don't have to shovel snow from a driveway that runs the whole length of the yard and makes a circle in back. In autumn, I don't have to rake the leaves from several big shade trees that spread their branches above the roof. One final point, in summer

fresh flowers make me sneeze. But, the family turned into an army and marched over me.

43   There was no problem in selling our house. People came running like kids rushing to an ice cream truck. I wondered what was so special about living outside New York City if so many people took pleasure in living in it.

44   I can't claim that I wasn't happy when we moved into the new house at 50 Bay Shore Street. I thought it would be pleasant to sit in the yard and watch the grass grow in the summer. I was wrong. When grass grows, you don't watch it; you cut it!

45   That yard was as long and wide as a field. In fact, it looked like a large hay farm. I mentioned to Alice that our son, John, was strong and healthy enough to cut the grass. I even suggested that we ask him to. She refused to consider this answer to the problem. She only replied that John ranked third in his class this year, and that he had to study during the summer to keep up his grades. I also wanted him to go to college and get a degree, didn't I? Well, either he didn't study much or else he did it in the car because nothing on earth could keep him in the house. When I once suggested he help out, he lifted the rake, gazed into the air for a few seconds, then asked if his mother had told me that he ranked third in his class and that he was supposed to study in order to keep up his grades? At this point I almost broke down.

46   And then there was the garden. It was on a hill—more like a small mountain—and the soil was as hard as rock. When it rained, the water washed the plants down to the kitchen door. In the morning after each storm, I picked them up and started the garden over

67

A12

again. I must have walked miles on my hands and knees. It got to be a game between me and the weather, one that I knew I'd never win.

47   This state of affairs was not the sort of thing that could go on long. And it didn't. Within a month my wife had another idea. One night when I had fallen into my chair in front of the fireplace (I had cut the wood for it that afternoon), she handed me a picture of a village in the mountains. "Doesn't that look pretty, Henry?" she asked. "All of those white houses look so clean and bright."

48   I was so tired my eyes were crossed, but I managed to express some half-hearted opinion. Then my face fell, and my heart stood still. I suddenly remembered that our house was green. I'm certain at that moment I would have agreed to visit the moon or an island in the middle of the ocean; but it wasn't necessary.

49   My wife put her arm across my shoulder. I waited. "Don't you think, dear," she said, "that it would be a nice idea for us to paint the outside of the house? We can save money if we do it ourselves."

50   Now, I think that a man should learn to control himself; but I had had it. I fell forward with my head in my hands and this time I did start to cry.

51   As I drove home from work the next night, I thought things over. Here I was in the United States of America, a free man, and a good husband who tried to provide for his family. Yet, I didn't even have time to read the news or watch a ball game any more. The reason was obvious; I was a slave to my house. As I drove through the gate to the house I saw smoke coming out of the windows. I ran up the steps and through the front door. Alice caught me in the hall.

52   "It's nothing important," she said. "I only tried to turn on the furnace to get heat, but something was wrong with it. I'm afraid there's oil all over the kitchen floor. I can't cook in there or clean up the mess until it cools off. You'll have to take us out to dinner and then fix it. Now I think you'll need to paint the inside of the house as soon as you finish painting the outside."

53   Well, sir, I made up my mind. I loved my wife and my son and daughter; but the house was killing me. I realized that my life was being destroyed! I turned around and drove away, as fast as the law allowed. I've had my bed here in the office ever since. I just send my wife a check every month.

54   Sometimes the family comes to visit me. I miss them and I'm not really happy living alone; but it's either the house or me. So far, the house is winning.

SKILL GROUP C

COMPREHENSION AND ANALYSIS SKILLS

I. Language Analysis

Discuss the meaning of the following words and phrases:

Par. 36: (a) been in on it . . .	Par. 39: (a) you can't beat
(b) wild as an Indian	City Hall
Par. 37: (a) something was up	Par. 40: (a) house of her dreams
Par. 38: (a) look worn and shaky . . .	(b) a minute's peace
(b) look into	

A13

Par. 42: (a) marched over me
Par. 45: (a) ranked third in his
class . . . (b) gazed . . .
(c) broke down

Par. 47: (a) state of affairs
Par. 48: (a) half-hearted

II. Content Analysis

Answer these questions.

1. To 'narrate' means 'to tell someone.' This story is called a 'narrative' because:
( ) it tells you how to buy a house; ( ) the man tells you what happened to him;
( ) the wife tells her husband she wants to move.

2. What did the man lose by moving into the country? ( ) time to relax; ( ) his love of the city; ( ) fresh air and exercise.

3. Did his wife say she wanted to move for her own sake, or the children's? _____

4. Who ended up doing all the work around the house? _____

III. Vocabulary Usage

A. Draw a line to connect each word on the left with the one on the right that has the same meaning.

require	take away
seek	hit
several	need
remove	sure
larger	a few
strike	look for
certain	bigger
attempt	try

B. These words have several meanings. Use them to complete the following sentences. Each may be used twice.

degree	view
condition	suit
proper	minute

1. The thermometer showed that the temperature had risen one _____ since noon.

2. _____ means very small.

3. Visitors must _____ newborn babies through a window.

69

A14

4. Sailors must _____ themselves to the pitching of their ships by the sea.

5. Jerry has a _____ in accounting.

6. I think this color will _____ me.

7. The _____ to the east is spectacular; you can see the sun rise over the plains.

8. The football player was in poor _____; he hadn't practiced in 2 weeks.

9. It's not _____ to wear blue jeans to the opera.

10. This machine can produce 40 cardboard boxes a _____ .

11. The union is facing a law _____ for breaking its work contract.

12. If he had put up a _____ fight he might still be living in his city home.

C. Underline the word that best completes the sentence.

1. The reporter was (hoping, hopping) to question the criminal on his reasons for killing his gentle old uncle.

2. The zoo paid him $2,000 for (bagging, begging) a rare black leopard.

3. The young boy was (baiting, biting) his fishhook with a worm.

4. While Clyde was (robing, robbing) the bank, Bonnie waited in the car.

5. David is (whining, willing) to take you to the airport, if you decide to fly.

6. Children were punished by (canning, caning) in pioneer schools.

7. This knife needs (whetting, wetting).

8. Tonight we are (dining, dinning) at a French restaurant.

9. (Homing, Humming) pigeons can be used to carry messages.

10. The firemen were (fitting, fighting) to save the burning building.

IV. Supplementary Discussion

1. Does this sound as if it could be a true story?

2. Do you think the man was too easy on his children?

3. Do you think most parents do too much or not enough for their children?

70

A15

VOCABULARY DRILL

---

1. To allow is to (1) permit (2) stop (3) solve (4) shine (5) arrange

2. To ask is to (1) purchase (2) inquire (3) provide (4) give money (5) deny

3. To attempt is to (1) fail (2) succeed (3) try (4) win (5) befuddle

4. To beat is to (1) race (2) hit (3) allow (4) sink (5) eat

5. Certain means (1) detain (2) important (3) proud (4) sure (5) wealthy

6. A circle is a (1) square (2) balloon (3) perfectly round shape (4) planet (5) group

7. Clean means (1) wise (2) healthy (3) without (4) debased (5) not dirty

8. Condition means (1) worthwhile (2) repetition (3) slovenly (4) boundary (5) state

9. Country means (1) land without cities (2) city (3) continent (4) township (5) western

10. Degree means (1) a lot of questions (2) alert people (3) unit of measure of angle (4) cold (5) amount of depth

11. To demand is to (1) request strongly (2) curse (3) wish (4) detest (5) offer to give

12. To desire is to (1) demand (2) wish (3) say (4) hope (5) fear

13. The sun rises in the (1) east (2) west (3) summer (4) north (5) south

14. Gentle means (1) gay and laughing (2) hard and coarse (3) soft and mild (4) sad and tearful (5) clean hands

15. Home means (1) run (2) abode (3) neighborhood (4) family (5) place

16. Larger means (1) heavier (2) smaller (3) bigger (4) tenant (5) smarter

17. Light means (1) illumination (2) wrong (3) heavy (4) fortunate (5) powerful

18. To lose is to (1) untie (2) win something (3) be defeated (4) be near (5). gain weight

19. To find the length or weight of something is to (1) estimate (2) examine (3) measure (4) allow (5) guess

20. 1/60th of an hour is (1) one hour (2) one day (3) one minute (4) one year (5) one half-minute

21. To offer means to (1) decide (2) refuse (3) suggest (4) obey (5) expel

22. Pleasure means (1) good feeling (2) wealthy (3) pain (4) wisdom (5) discomfort

A16

23. Practice is to (1) do practical thinking (2) have a good talk (3) take for granted (4) play jokes on people (5) repeat some exercise to build up skill in it

24. Produce means (1) characterize (2) propose (3) destroy (4) swell (5) bring forth

25. Proper means (1) witty (2) correct (3) neat (4) necessary (5) handsome

26. To question means to (1) answer (2) unveil (3) inquire or ask (4) disperse with (5) engage in

27. To refuse is to (1) forget (2) reject (3) say good-by (4) do it again (5) use

28. To remove is to (1) change places (2) renew (3) deny (4) take away (5) keep in one spot

29. To require is to (1) believe (2) release (3) demand (4) decide (5) ask

30. Sea refers to (1) using your eyes (2) ocean (3) spiritual communication (4) part of the year (5) a seal

31. To seek means to (1) settle (2) find (3) search (4) swim at great depths (5) withdraw

32. Several means (1) too many (2) others (3) a few (4) to cut (5) divided

33. Smoking means (1) to give out smoke (2) fire (3) cigarette (4) cooking (5) needlework

34. Soil means (1) air (2) path (3) dirt (4) ship (5) clean

35. Strike means (1) to run (2) to hit (3) to argue (4) to star (5) to cross the road

36. Suggest means (1) to order (2) a small book (3) to hint (4) an illness (5) a record

37. A number of things used together is (1) an arrow (2) a suit (3) a minimum (4) a dress (5) wood

38. A child's father's brother is (1) his aunt (2) his step-brother (3) no relationship (4) his uncle (5) his friend

39. To view is to (1) live (2) see (3) move (4) hear (5) be watched

40. To be wild is to be (1) tame (2) willful (3) uncontrollable (4) wishful (5) a child

A17

COMMUNICATION SKILLS LEVEL II

In Communication Skills Level I you learned to use the 1,000 words most often used in the English language. This Level, Level II, contains the next 1,000 most common words. When you finish Level II you will have used and studied 2,000 different words from the language you read and speak every day.

II

73

A18

WORD ATTACK SKILLS

How to Make Verbs

SECTION 1   --See if you can remember how to add the suffix

"ing" to long vowel and short vowel words.

1) A suffix is a group of letters that can be

added to the end of a word: "ing" is

a suffix.

2) To add the suffix "ing" to a word that ends

with a silent "e," drop the "e" and add "ing."

EXAMPLE: tăm$\not{e}$ + ĭng = tām + ĭng = tāmĭng

3) To add the suffix "ing" to a short vowel word,

you must have 2 consonants before adding "ing."

a.   If a short vowel word already ends with

2 consonants, just add "ing."

EXAMPLE: pŭll + ĭng = pŭllĭng

b.   If a short vowel word ends with one

consonant, add another consonant before

adding "ing."

EXAMPLE: bĕg + g + ĭng = bĕggĭng

74

A19

4) There are 2 parts to a word ending with

a suffix: a <u>root</u> and a <u>suffix</u>.

EXAMPLE: rop$\not{e}$ + ĭng = rōpĭng

"rope" is the <u>root</u>

"ing" is the <u>suffix.</u>

SECTION 2

--Another suffix is "ed." You can add "ed" to a

word the same way you added "ing."

EXAMPLE: hōp$\not{e}$ + ĭng = hōp + ĭng = hōp<u>ing</u>

hōp$\not{e}$ + ed = hōp + ed = hōp<u>ed</u>

kĭll + ed = kĭlled

--Notice how the "ed" at the end of a word sometimes

sounds like a "t" and sometimes like a "d."

--<u>Circle</u> the words ending with suffixes.

bed	baking	sting	hope	voted
piling	rule	wiped	nap	canned
bit	bin	biting	bringing	spin
sitting	patted	getting	win	craving

75

A20

SECTION 3   --When you add "ed" to a root word ending with

a silent "e," drop the silent "e" and add "ed."

EXAMPLE: dat$\bar{e}$ + $\breve{e}$d = d$\bar{a}$t + $\breve{e}$d = d$\bar{a}$t$\breve{e}$d

--Work with your group to do 4 things to the following

words:

1)   Pronounce each one;

2)   Mark the vowels;

■

3)   Add the suffix "ed"; and

4)   Tell whether the "ed" sounds like a

"t," "d," or "ed."

w$\bar{i}$pe ----- __wiped__   t   spike----- _____   ___
tam$e$----- __t$\bar{a}$med__   d   note------ __noted__   __ed__
bale------ _____   __   cube------ _____   __
smile---- _____   __   rate------ _____   __
space---- _____   __   bake------ _____   __

--Check your answers with your group and

your monitor.

SECTION 4   --To add the suffix "ed" to a short vowel word,

you must have 2 consonants before adding "ed."

A21

--If a short vowel word already ends with 2

consonants, just add "ed."

EXAMPLE: tălk + ed = tălked

--Work with your group to do 4 things to the

following words:

     1)   Pronounce each one;

     2)   Underline the consonants the word

          ends with;

     3)   Add the suffix "ed"; and

     4)   Tell whether the "ed" is pronounced as

          "t" or "d."

rock -----rocked   t   pull -----_____ ___

spill-----_____ ___   pick -----_____ ___

smell----_____ ___   walk-----_____ ___

B1

Appendix B

Paper Forms used by PMI/MS

B2

<u>SCORING FORM</u>

NAME _____   SEQUENCE NO: _____

DATE _____

Scoring: exemptions:____

items

[1][2][3][4][5][6][7][8][9][10]
[11][12][13][14][15][16][17][18][19][20]
[21][22][23][24][25][26][27][28][29][30]
[31][32][33][34][35][36][37][38][39][40]
[41][42][43][44][45][46][47][48][49][50]
[51][52][53][54][55][56][57][58][59][60]
[61][62][63][64][65][66][67][68][69][70]
[71][72][73][74][75][76][77][78][79][80]
[81][82][83][84][85][86][87][88][89][90]
[91][92][93][94][95][96][97][98][99][100]

<u>passes</u>

[1][2][3][4][5]

Assignment:

Student gets all items right: _____

Student uses up all passes: _____

Supervised by: _____

B3
<u>READER'S EVALUATION FORM</u>

NAME _____   SEQUENCE NO: _____

DATE _____

This reading should be:

      kept in the program ☐   ☐ not kept in the program

     Reasons:

_____
_____
_____
_____
_____
_____
_____
_____
_____
_____
_____
_____
_____
_____
_____
_____
_____
_____
_____

B4

Student Activity Checklist

SEQ. NO.	S/I	LOCATION	PROCEDURES	Done

Teacher Activity Checklist

| SEQ. NO. | SCORING | | | ASSIGNMENT | | PROCEDURES |
	ITMS	PASS	EXMP	IF 'A'	IF 'B'	
						B5

B6

TEACHING FORM						
	SCORING			ASSIGNMENT		
SEQ. NO.	ITMS	PASS	EXMP	IF 'A'	IF 'B'	PROCEDURES
360	18	3	1	370	350	Copy information onto Scoring Form; Student Manual procedures; be sure Student does items in correct order; correct and score each item. [Sec. 2 = items 1-9; Sec. 3 = 10-18]

	crave	----- craving	5	drive	----- driving
1	tame	----- taming	6	fake	----- faking
2	rise	----- rising	7	vote	----- voting
3	save	----- saving	8	tune	----- tuning
4	bake	----- baking	9	wave	----- waving

	rule	----- ruling	14	fade	----- fading
10	date	----- dating	15	wipe	----- wiping
11	pave	----- paving	16	stake	----- staking
12	bale	----- baling	17	rise	----- rising
13	tune	----- tuning	18	note	----- noting

83

C1

Appendix C

A Sample Student Activity Checklist

(For MIND text in Appendix A)

C2

Student Activity Checklist

SEQ. NO.	S/I	LOCATION	PROCEDURES	Done
350	I	pp. 32-38, Sec. 1,2,4,6,9	Study only; do not mark the exercises	
360	S	MIND, pp. 32-33, Sec.2&3	Write each word on a PAD adding "ing" to it; show each answer to your Teacher.	
370	S	MIND, pp. 33-34, Sec. 4&5	Write each word on a PAD adding "ing" to it.	
380	S	MIND, pp. 35-36, Sec. 6&7	Re-write each word by doubling the final consonant and adding "ing"; on a PAD.	
390	S	MIND, pp. 36-37, Sec. 8	Write each word on a PAD adding "ing" to it.	
400	S	MIND, pp. 37-38, Sec. 9&10	Follow MIND procedures on a PAD.	
410	I	MIND, pp. 39-40, Vocab.	Study words and meanings.	
420	I	MIND, pp. 40-42, Reading	Read.	
430	I	Reader Evaluation Form	Evaluate reading passage on pages 40-42.	

85

Note: Pages references under LOCATION refer to the pages numbers of the actual MIND text. Appendix A of the PMI/MS Manual in this book contains a representative passage of the MIND text, a passage beginning on page 32 of that book. In *Peer-Mediated Instruction,* this passage begins on page 232.

C3

Student Activity Checklist

SEQ. NO.	S/I	LOCATION	PROCEDURES	Done
440	S	MIND, pp. 39-40, Vocab.	Spell words as usual on a PAD.	
450	S	MIND, p. 43, Sec. III-A	Match words that mean the same on a PAD.	
460	S	MIND, pp. 43-44, Sec. B	Follow MIND procedures on a PAD.	
470	S	MIND, p. 44, Sec. C	Read each sentence using word that belongs.	
479	I	MIND, pp. 39-40, Vocab.	Study words AND meanings.	
480	S	MIND, pp. 45-46, Drill	Circle word that means the same.	
485	I	Criterion Review	Get Criterion Review form your Trainer.	
490	I	MIND, pp. 49-52, Sec. 1-4	Study and do exercises.	

D1

Appendix D

A Sample Teacher Activity Checklist

(For MIND Text in Appendix A)

D2

Teacher Activity Checklist

SEQ.NO.	SCORING			ASSIGNMENT		PROCEDURES
	ITMS	PASS	EXMP	IF 'A'	IF 'B'	
360	18	3	1	370	350	Copy information onto Scoring Form; Student should follow Student Manual procedures; be sure Student does items in correct order; correct and score each item. [Sec. 2 = items 1-9; Sec. 3 = 10-18]
370	16	5	1	380	380	Follow Standard procedures (see PROCEDURES on Seq. No. 360 above for more information on Standard procedures.) [Sec. 4 = items 1-7; Sec. 5 = 8-16]
380	18	5	2	390	390	Standard procedures (see #50). [Sec. 6 = items 1-9; Sec. 7 = 10-18]
390	13	5	1	400	400	Standard procedures.
400	19	5	2	410	410	Standard procedures [Sec. 9 = 1-14; Sec. 10 = 15-19].
440	40	5	4	450	450	Follow Spelling procedures (read each word to the Student; he should spell words on a PAD; if he misspells it, correct it on the PAD; if he gives up, spell it for him on the PAD; if he gets it right, check item off on the Scoring Form.)

D3

Teacher Activity Checklist

| SEQ. NO. | SCORING | | | ASSIGNMENT | | PROCEDURES |
	ITMS	PASS	EXMP	IF 'A'	IF 'B'	
450	8	5	0	460	460	Standard procedures.
460	12	5	1	470	470	Standard procedures.
470	10	5	1	480	480	Standard procedures.
480	40	3	4	485	479	Standard procedures.

E1

Appendix E

Correct Answer Forms

(For MIND text in Appendix A)

E2

CORRECT ANSWERS

No.: 360

	crave	craving	5	drive	driving
1	tame	taming	6	fake	faking
2	rise	rising	7	vote	voting
3	save	saving	8	tune	tuning
4	bake	baking	9	wave	waving

	rule	ruling	14	fade	fading
10	date	dating	15	wipe	wiping
11	pave	paving	16	stake	staking
12	bale	baling	17	rise	rising
13	tune	tuning	18	note	noting

E3

No.: __370__

lick-----licking   4   pick----- picking

1 sell ----- selling   5   truck---- trucking

2 stack---- stacking   6   pack----- packing

3 pull----- pulling   7   mock---- mocking

pick----- picking   12 bill----- billing

8   dock----- docking   13 stalk---- stalking

9   tell----- telling   14 will----- willing

10 rock---- rocking   15 lock----- locking

11 fall----- falling   16 buck----- bucking

E4

CORRECT ANSWERS

No.: __380__

---

lĕt----- lĕttĭng   5   spot----- spotting

1   scan---- scanning   6   dig----- digging

2   snap---- snapping   7   hog----- hogging

3   snag---- snagging   8   mob----- mobbing

4   wet----- wetting   9   rot----- rotting

păn----- pănnĭng   14   chop----- chopping

10   nag----- nagging   15   tan----- tanning

11   trap----- trapping   16   sun----- sunning

12   cut----- cutting   17   snip---- snipping

13   mop----- mopping   18   grab--- grabbing

E5

CORRECT ANSWERS

No.: ___390___

bĕg----- bĕggĭng	4	pack-------- packing
1 set----- setting	5	strip------- stripping
2 wade--- wading	6	mop------- mopping
3 get----- getting	7	smell------ smelling

lock---- locking	10	tan-------- tanning
8 save---- saving	11	park------ parking
9 chat---- chatting	12	fade------ fading

94

E6

CORRECT ANSWERS

No.: ___400___

pĕckĭng----- _pĕck_   4 spanning----- _span_

1 filling------ _fill_   5 snagging----- _snag_

2 docking----- _dock_   6 trapping----- _trap_

3 stalking----- _stalk_   7 cutting------ _cut_

8 telling------ _tell_   12 mopping---- _mop_

9 ruling------ _rule_   13 fading------ _fade_

10 dating------ _date_   14 wiping----- _wipe_

11 paving------ _pave_

hŏppĭng------- _hŏp_   17 biting------- _bite_

15 hoping-------- _hope_   18 letting------ _let_

16 lacking------- _lack_   19 tanning----- _tan_

E7

CORRECT ANSWERS

No.: ___450___

1	require	— need	take away
2	seek	— look for	hit
3	several	— a few	need
4	remove	— take away	sure
5	larger	— bigger	a few
6	strike	— hit	look for
7	certain	— sure	bigger
8	attempt	— try	try

E8

---

1. The thermometer showed that the temperature had risen one _degree_ since noon.

2. _Minute_ means very small.

3. Visitors must _view_ newborn babies through a window.

4. Sailors must **condition** themselves to the pitching of their ships by the sea.

5. Jerry has a _degree_ in accounting.

6. I think this color will _suit_ me.

7. The _view_ to the east is spectacular; you can see the sun rise over the plains.

8. The football player was in poor _condition_; he hadn't practiced in 2 weeks.

9. It's not _proper_ to wear blue jeans to the opera.

10. This machine can produce 40 cardboard boxes a _minute_.

11. The union is facing a law _suit_ for breaking its work contract.

12. If he had put up a _proper_ fight he might still be living in his city home.

E9

CORRECT ANSWERS

No.: _470_

---

1. The reporter was (hoping, hopping) to question the criminal on his reasons for killing his gentle old uncle.

2. The zoo paid him $2,000 for (bagging, begging) a rare black leopard.

3. The young boy was (baiting, biting) his fishhook with a worm.

4. While Clyde was (robing, robbing) the bank, Bonnie waited in the car.

5. David is (whining, willing) to take you to the airport, if you decide to fly.

6. Children were punished by (canning, caning) in pioneer schools.

7. This knife needs (whetting, wetting).

8. Tonight we are (dining, dinning) at a French restaurant.

9. (Homing, Humming) pigeons can be used to carry messages.

10. The firemen were (fitting, fighting) to save the burning building.

E10

CORRECT ANSWERS

No.: 480

1. To allow is to (1) **permit** (2) stop (3) solve (4) shine (5) arrange

2. To ask is to (1) purchase (2) **inquire** (3) provide (4) give money (5) deny

3. To attempt is to (1) fail (2) succeed (3) **try** (4) win (5) befuddle

4. To beat is to (1) race (2) **hit** (3) allow (4) sink (5) eat

5. Certain means (1) detain (2) important (3) proud (4) **sure** (5) wealthy

6. A circle is a (1) square (2) balloon (3) **perfectly round shape** (4) planet (5) group

7. Clean means (1) wise (2) healthy (3) without (4) debased (5) **not dirty**

8. Condition means (1) worthwhile (2) repetition (3) slovenly (4) boundary (5) **state**

9. Country means (1) **land without cities** (2) city (3) continent (4) township (5) western

10. Degree means (1) a lot of questions (2) alert people (3) **unit of measure of angle** (4) cold (5) amount of depth

11. To demand is to (1) **request strongly** (2) curse (3) wish (4) detest (5) offer to give

12. To desire is to (1) demand (2) **wish** (3) say (4) hope (5) fear

13. The sun rises in the (1) **east** (2) west (3) summer (4) north (5) south

14. Gentle means (1) gay and laughing (2) hard and coarse (3) **soft and mild** (4) sad and tearful (5) clean hands

15. Home means (1) run (2) abode (3) neighborhood (4) **family** (5) place

16. Larger means (1) heavier (2) smaller (3) **bigger** (4) tenant (5) smarter

17. Light means (1) **illumination** (2) wrong (3) heavy (4) fortunate (5) powerful

18. To lose is to (1) untie (2) win something (3) **be defeated** (4) be near (5) gain weight

19. To find the length or weight of something is to (1) estimate (2) examine (3) **measure** (4) allow (5) guess

20. 1/60th of an hour is (1) one hour (2) one day (3) **one minute** (4) one year (5) one half-minute

21. To offer means to (1) decide (2) refuse (3) **suggest** (4) obey (5) expel

22. Pleasure means (1) **good feeling** (2) wealthy (3) pain (4) wisdom (5) discomfort

274

Peer-Mediated Instruction

E11

CORRECT ANSWERS

No.: 480 (cont.)

23. Practice is to (1) do practical thinking (2) have a good talk (3) take for granted (4) play jokes on people (5) repeat some exercise to build up skill in it

24. Produce means (1) characterize (2) propose (3) destroy (4) swell (5) bring forth

25. Proper means (1) witty (2) correct (3) neat (4) necessary (5) handsome

26. To question means to (1) answer (2) unveil (3) inquire or ask (4) disperse with (5) engage in

27. To refuse is to (1) forget (2) reject (3) say good-by (4) do it again (5) use

28. To remove is to (1) change places (2) renew (3) deny (4) take away (5) keep in one spot

29. To require is to (1) believe (2) release (3) demand (4) decide (5) ask

30. Sea refers to (1) using your eyes (2) ocean (3) spiritual communication (4) part of the year (5) a seal

31. To seek means to (1) settle (2) find (3) search (4) swim at great depths (5) withdraw

32. Several means (1) too many (2) others (3) a few (4) to cut (5) divided

33. Smoking means (1) to give out smoke (2) fire (3) cigarette (4) cooking (5) needlework

34. Soil means (1) air (2) path (3) dirt (4) ship (5) clean

35. Strike means (1) to run (2) to hit (3) to argue (4) to star (5) to cross the road

36. Suggest means (1) to order (2) a small book (3) to hint (4) an illness (5) a record

37. A number of things used together is (1) an arrow (2) a suit (3) a minimum (4) a dress (5) wood

38. A child's father's brother is (1) his aunt (2) his step-brother (3) no relationship (4) his uncle (5) his friend

39. To view is to (1) live (2) see (3) move (4) hear (5) be watched

40. To be wild is to be (1) tame (2) willful (3) uncontrollable (4) wishful (5) a child

100

Acknowledgments

THE SPONSORS

International Business Machines Corporation
Holt, Rinehart and Winston, Inc.
Horace Mann-Lincoln Institute
American Telephone and Telegraph Company
New York Telephone Company
South Central Bell Telephone Company
Jackson Public Schools, Jackson, Mississippi
New World Foundation
Teachers College, Columbia University

THE PARTICIPANTS,
in order of their appearance, to each of whom my deepest thanks are offered

Edward N. Adams	IBM Corporation
Francis A. J. Ianni	Horace Mann-Lincoln Institute
Jerry Barney Alice Cooper Bonita Leeds Deborah Stevens	Teachers College, Columbia University

276

Martha Froelich James Brown Kevin Lloyd	P. S. 129, New York City
John Teem	Xerox Corporation
G. T. Bowden Charles Sherrard	American Telephone and Telegraph Company
F. Bruce Hinkel Rita Kenny Millie Torres	New York Telephone
Robert Daly Beatrice Dilworth Narcissa Eastmond Samuel Rollins Angelo Sanchez	New York Telephone
Barbara Theobald Virginia Vida	Holt, Rinehart and Winston, Inc.
Hugh Jacks	South Central Bell
Brandon Sparkman	Jackson Public Schools
Mildred Hust Margaret Allen	Jackson Public Schools
Charlene Sharman Poesie Smith Rosa Twyner	Jackson Public Schools
Arthur and Susan Klein Louis Forsdale Paul Kelberg	friends
Ilene Kornblath	who witnessed the Last Word

About the Author

Peter S. Rosenbaum is an Associate Professor of Linguistics and Education at Teachers College, Columbia University. He is a graduate of Wesleyan University and holds a Ph.D. in linguistics from the Massachusetts Institute of Technology.

Dr. Rosenbaum is the Director of the Center for the Study of Systems and Technology in Education of the Horace Mann-Lincoln Institute.